Preston Welles II

Miguel Sinnott

Edited by Meaghan Wagner of New York Book Editors

Book Cover Design by ebooklaunch.com

CONTENTS

Preface

Dear Reader,

Thank you very much for purchasing my novel. As I attempt to build a career as an author, I truly appreciate your supporting my work. I would be grateful if you left a review of this story – my second attempt at writing a full-length novel – so I may continue to improve my craft.

Sincerely,

Miguel Sinnott

1

DARK PASSAGE

I was in a jam – that was bad enough. I was battered from top to toe – that was even worse. I was being hunted by brutes with big fists and bigger guns – that was worse still.

Why was I staggering through these sordid streets, bruised, bleeding, burdened by blows and blasts and betrayals? Simple – I didn't learn my lesson the last time I investigated other people's affairs. Getting too curious brought me a heap of trouble before, but this mushy mind of mine made me think doing the same thing this time would lead to different results. Dopes never learn.

What a mess I was. My body felt like a slab of steak after a turn with the tenderizer. My mind felt like a canister of Pillsbury Doughboy that had been left in a hot trunk. And my soul? Skip it.

A bullet breezed by my head and off a brick wall to my right. They were catching up to me again. I lurched along the sidewalk, groping for lampposts and fence pales. I was as graceful as a drunk on Cinco de Mayo.

There was the Duke's Hall. Good old theater. Grand old theater. I owed a lot of beatdowns to this place.

A teenager slouched in the ticket booth. Monkey-shaped ears as big as bowling balls were crammed under a bucket hat. Skin mottled with food coloring flaked off his lips like peeling paint. A slender nose stuck out like an elephant's trunk and looked like it would flap in high wind.

"Scan your ticket," he squeaked.

"I don't have a ticket, Dumbo. Some guys are after me. I need inside."

"Scan your ticket. The doors only open if you scan your ticket."

"I told you I don't have a ticket."

"Scan your ticket."

There wasn't time or sense in standing here, so I crept into the dark passage between the theater and the building directly east. I had been through a lot of dark passages lately, a lot of dusky chambers and dismal hallways and gloomy courts. There was nothing new there. It came with the territory of being a nosy stooge.

This dark passage granted access to the stage door, before which another teenager, dressed in a scarlet uniform, stood atop five concrete stairs.

"Want some dough?" I asked.

"Dough, huh?" he smirked while his eyes explored my buffeted carcass. "You ask me if I want dough? This ain't Christmas, so that means you want a favor. I don't like doing guys favors, Jack. Especially ones that been roughed up like you have."

I pulled a hundred dollar bill out of my pocket and showed it to him.

"I'll be going in that door, and you'll be following me inside. You'll be locking the door from the inside and not answering it, even if you hear guys knocking out here. Got all that?"

"Who's your playmates, Jack?" he sneered.

"A couple of rough guys. You wouldn't like their company."

"You'd be surprised, Jack. I like lots of peoples' company."

"Take my word for it."

"I don't know that I will, Jack. Your playmates wouldn't happen to be cops, would they, Jack?"

"Do you want the dough, or not?"

He pushed his tongue between his teeth, like a snake. "I want the dough, Jack."

After the kid did what I asked, I handed him his coin.

"Thanks."

"Thanks to you, Jack," he tipped his cap. "Enjoy the show."

This corridor led to a push door; behind that was the theater itself. I didn't want to go backstage, just yet. I needed time to think. I needed time to compose myself. I needed time to breathe without worrying where the next bullet would go or where the next punch would land.

An orchestra had just commenced the second movement of Beethoven's *Seventh Symphony* while I searched for an open chair. Going up these gradual stairs felt like climbing Mount Everest with a mule on my back.

I found an absent fifth chair nine rows up and struggled into the seat and panted like a horse crossing the Sahara. The guys after me weren't likely to listen to Dumbo's demand to scan their tickets, but no one had followed me inside, yet. Maybe they hadn't seen me duck in here. Maybe they thought I was still stumbling through those streets.

But Beethoven. The music suited my mood – ominous, foreboding, fatalistic. Funny thing, my taking refuge in this cathedral of art. I snickered at the irony, chuckled at it, roared at it in sardonic laughter. Fitting this theater would shield me now, because this is where it all began, between these walls, under this roof, above this stage.

See, a week ago, everything was peachy. Denis Bucy had just published my second novel, *Coquettes and Concord*, a historical novel set during the American Revolution which combined a captivating narrative with a subtle exposition of who actually caused the revolution, and why. Early returns suggested it might eclipse the popularity of my first book, and I was in the mood for mirth.

My destination? This same Duke's Hall for a vaudeville production of George M. Cohan songs, followed by Tchaikovsky's *Swan Lake*. And it didn't take me long to decide I liked the setup. After "Only Forty Five Minutes From Broadway", a brunette with raven-colored hair in a sweeping white gown appeared for the beginning of "So Long Mary."

That face. Oh, mercy, that face. The hazel eyes. The gentle cheeks. The luscious lips. Had I seen a prettier one before? I doubted it.

As the song was concluding, something tapped my right arm, and a guy on my right grinned expectantly. A guy with a gut as big as a bosu ball and carrot-colored hair drizzled with dandruff and gorilla-shaped teeth that looked like they could grind through granite. Little white sacs of spit had accumulated on the corners of his mouth.

"Ever tried aardvark?" he asked as spittle flew from his lips like a white pebble launched from a slingshot. His light, warbling voice reminded me of a whistle.

"Huh?"

"Aardvark. Have you ever tried it?"

"I have it every year for my birthday."

"Would you say it's less gamey than squirrel, or are the two similar?"

"What?"

"Squirrel. How does aardvark compare to squirrel?"

"I don't recommend either."

"No? That's curious. I've indulged both several times and loved every bite of each. Between aardvark, squirrel, and beaver, which one is the smokiest?"

I stood up. "I can either watch these dames, or listen to you. I'll take the dames."

"Oh, pardon my loquacity," the guy tittered, sending spit onto the stage and putting a pudgy paw on my elbow. "I am wont to share my tastes with fellow patrons of Western art, only sometimes I cannot contain myself. My name is Dudley

Ridgley. You intimate you like these 'dames'? What is your opinion of the brunette?"

"I give her an A+. That's why I'm moving to where I can get a better glimpse of her."

"Pray remain hither, and let me introduce you after the show! She is my niece. Very beautiful girl. Very remarkable girl. How old are you?"

"Twenty-three."

"She is twenty-two. And what is your name?"

“Preston Welles.”

“Preston Welles?” Ridgley’s tiny eyes widened. “As in, the author?”

“As in, the author.”

"Oh, all the better!" he giggled as spit began to trickle down his chin. "She naturally resists my matchmaking, but she will not say no to a sterling artist as yourself. Superlative, brilliant, dashing young novelist at her dressing room door? She will say yes, yes, yes, yes!"

"I say yes to watching this without any more interruptions from you."

"To be sure," Ridgley clapped like a seal. "A thousand thanks for your conversation."

How a guy that looked like him could have a niece that looked like her was beyond me, but I wasn't going to waste any energy trying to figure it out.

Cohan's songs gave way to *Swan Lake*. Prince Sigfield and his companions went to the lake. The swan with the crown – Ridgley's niece - became Odette. Rothbart tricked Prince Sigfield with Odile. Prince Sigfield realized his error and pledged to die with Odette. Rothbart perished with the breaking of the spell. The lovers ascended united. Exeunt.

Ridgley fidgeted increasingly, climaxing with his emitting mirthful grunts, like a pig wallowing in the mire. Before the scarlet curtain had even dropped, he was tugging at my elbow like an eager child.

"Make haste, Welles," he commanded breathily, "lest the swan princess ascend afore we pay her our tributes."

I followed Ridgley's waddling around the stage and past stage workers scurrying around like ants and by some of Odette's swan maidens. They'd be a suitable backup plan, if they hadn't migrated by the time I'd seen Ridgley's niece.

At the end of the hall was the dressing room. Ridgley giggled some more and knocked with exuberance.

“Laura!” he pelted the door with spit. “Laura, I’ve someone to see you! Someone very important! Laura, you must see him! Laura, why don’t you answer me? What’s the matter?”

Finally, he noticed the paper taped to the door that read, in impeccable cursive, “Do Not Disturb Me.”

“What’s the meaning of this?” Ridgley fumed as he snatched the sheet and crumpled it with his plump fingers. “She wasn’t supposed to shut herself in. Laura, you’d better answer this door, do you hear? Answer this door!”

Fair as Laura looked from afar, the disappointment at not getting to meet her was minimal. I already had my mind back on that troupe of dames I'd seen coming over here, but when I turned my iPhone back on I saw it had received fifteen calls from a 505 number I didn't recognize. Then it started to ring.

I answered to a car’s engine running in the background. A few seconds later, somebody hung up.

"Someone calling you, handsome?" asked a swan maiden with brown hair.

"Just a prank call," I absently replied as I put the phone in silent mode. "It isn't a very interesting subject."

"What qualifies as interesting to you?" asked a short, comely one.

"Cute dames top the list."

"Like us?" asked a different swan maiden.

"Sure. The name is Welles."

"Are you related to Orson Welles?" asked the one with brown hair.

"No, but some people think so. I don't even like *Citizen Kane*

"Why not?" she pursued.

"It's too soporific."

"Soporific?" frowned the first one. "What's that?"

"A word for something sleep inducing."

"Are we soporific?" the short one smiled.

"I'd say you're right out of a fella's dreams."

"Aren't you a novelist?" the different one asked.

"From time to time. Some days I just read Shakespeare."

"Shakespeare?" one beamed. "Do you know *Othello*?"

"Sure. I pray you in your letters, when you shall these unlucky deeds relate, speak of me as I am. Nothing extenuate, nor set down aught in malice. Then must you speak of one that loved wisely, but too well; of one not easily jealous, but being wrought, perplexed in the extreme; of one whose hand, like the base Judean, threw a pearl away richer than all his tribe; of one whose subdued eyes, albeit unused to the melting mood, drop tears as fast as the Arabian trees their medicinable gum."

"And *The Merchant of Venice*?" asked the one with brown hair.

"The quality of mercy is not strain'd; it droppeth as the gentle rain from heaven upon the place beneath: it is twice bless'd; it blesseth him that gives, and him that takes: 'tis mightiest in the mightiest: it becomes the throned monarch better than his crown."

"We have crowns," the first one said. "Would you sign them?"

I did and took a group selfie and bid them good night. Making a habit of this was an appealing proposition.

On my way out, I noticed that same number had called five more times. I shrugged and shook my head. Some people can't take a hint.

2

OLD ACQUAINTANCES

The next afternoon, I was listening to Mozart's *Symphony No. 35* and scrawling out verse on those comely dames when somebody knocked. Two men were on the porch, and they didn't look like they were there to sell me something.

One guy was a little over fifty with a plain gray suit and black tie and a toothpick balanced between slightly yellow teeth. He had an ovular chin and suspicious gray eyes that only a cop would have. Beside him stood a bulky guy with matted brown hair and a dark brown suit. I'd seen them both before, on that eventful Christmas Eve of yore.

"Howdy, Welles," smirked the guy with the ovular chin. "The name's Malden. His name's Dixon. Figured I'd mention, in case you'd forgotten who we are. Mind if we come inside?"

"I mind."

"We'd prefer if you didn't, punk," Dixon sneered.

"I'd prefer if you left."

"Oh, but we're not going to," Malden said. "At least, not until you appease our curiosity. I told you before, Welles, that I love learning. I still love it. That's why we're here. We're gonna ask questions, and you're gonna give us answers."

"About what?" I frowned.

"You know what, punk," Dixon smiled nastily. "Your latest crime."

"I say this bird's trying to play dumb," said Malden. "That's why he's running with this malarkey about us not having a right to come in. As if we didn't."

"Yeah, as if we didn't," Dixon chortled. "Don't you know, punk? We're public servants. We can do whatever we want, especially to a punk like you that weaseled out of the chair."

With that, he walloped me onto my back and followed Malden into the room. They looked it over thoroughly.

"Still not much of a setup," Malden said. "I figure with all the dough you been pulling in, you might spruce up the joint."

"I don't like it, either," Dixon decided. "The punk should get the chair just on account of his lousy taste."

"I must have done something serious to have you two lugs tramping around here without a warrant."

"The law doesn't need a warrant to bust in on a punk like you," Dixon declared.

"I figured you'd be a little somber, on account of your pal getting bumped off," Malden said. "But I don't see much emotion. I don't even see a tear."

"Why should he be sorry?" Dixon shrugged. "He did it and liked it."

"I didn't do anything."

"No?" Malden pretended to be in earnest. "We don't see it that way, do we, Dixon?"

"No," Dixon sneered. "We don't."

"Take it from me, Welles," Malden said. "Just tell us why you did it, sign a confession, and we'll go easy on you. We might even lobby on your behalf."

"You heard the man, punk," Dixon said. "Don't make this any harder than it needs to be. Why'd you do it, punk?"

"I don't know what you're talking about."

"A first class comedian, this guy," Malden snickered. "Always leaves them laughing, doesn't he? What about your pal? He laughing when you left him?"

"What pal?"

"You know what pal. The pal you bumped off last night."

"I didn't bump off anyone last night. I was at the Duke's Hall. The dames in the show can corroborate that."

"Oh, they can, can they?" Dixon sneered. "Ain't that real nice."

Malden nodded subtly at Dixon, and I was back on my back following another haymaker. Dixon yanked me to my feet and sent me backwards with a sharp jab. I slammed off the wall and dropped to the floor like a sack of apples.

“It goes like this,” Malden smirked. “A guy named Nigel Wilfred turned his coupe into a fireball last night. But before that, he got his brains beat out. But before that, he called your number twenty-two times. You answered one of the calls for thirty-five seconds. That strike you as odd, Welles?”

Nigel Wilfred. The name hit me over the back of the head like a mallet. It couldn’t be so.

“Nigel?” I mumbled, not believing what I heard. “He, he’s...”

“Sure, he’s dead,” Dixon snorted. “You sapped him and lit his car on fire with him inside.”

“You seem surprised, Welles,” Malden said. “If I didn’t know any better, I’d say it was genuine.”

“Maybe it is. Maybe the punk’s genuinely surprised we’re onto him so soon. Maybe the punk thought he’d have more time to squirrel away dough and beat it before we found out. But the punk was wrong. And there isn't going to be any Mike Carson to save the day with a screwy confession this time, is there, punk?"

Nigel and I had grown up together. After he went to New Hampshire for university, we had stayed in touch until he stopped returning messages six months back. The university said he had unenrolled but didn't know why, and none of our mutual acquaintances had even known he had unenrolled. His only living relative in Albuquerque, a crass and contemptible cousin named Patty, couldn't have cared less where he was, so I hadn't heard anything from him, or about him, until now.

I stared straight ahead in oblivion. The world was a murk of cruel mystery. A solitary sphere flitting through space, indifferent to sympathy or kindness or gentleness or love. The things and the people in it scoffed at my solitude with flippant disregard and chilly nonchalance.

Beyond that, I couldn't see anything except the steamy film that was forming over my eyes. I tried to rub it away while looking at the floor.

"Ready to talk now, Welles?" Malden inquired.

I didn't say anything.

"Why'd you do it?"

"Get out of my sight."

"That wasn't a very considerate answer. Consider amending it, or I might ask Dixon here to teach you some manners."

"Leave me alone."

Malden sighed smugly, then raised his eyebrows, which was the prompt for Dixon to taze me. I was too engrossed absorbing the shockwaves of what I had just learned to notice anything beyond an extremely sharp sensation of pain radiating from head to toe.

"Looks like we're going to headquarters," Malden remarked as I writhed on the rug. "Cuff this crumb when he gets through wriggling. As far as the department's concerned, he bumped off Wilfred."

3

A ROOM WITHOUT A VIEW

The ride to the station whisked me by places and things I'd seen a thousand times, but they didn't seem the same. Something about them was different. Something about them was missing.

Nothing would ever be the same, with what I knew now. Nothing could ever be the same, with what I knew now.

The police station lobby was cold and unwelcoming. A guard looked me over thoroughly, like he was trying to remember who I was. When he remembered, he snickered.

"Decided to come back, huh, Welles? Why so? Did you get to longing for our hospitality? Or is it that criminals like you just can't stay away long?"

"I'm no criminal."

"Oh yes, you are. Just because you got off last time doesn't mean you're not a criminal. It means you got lucky. You're not getting lucky this time."

"This sweetheart bumped off Wilfred," Malden informed the guard. "We tried to get answers in his place, but he wasn't feeling cooperative."

"Is that so?" the guard sneered. "You just can't seem to help yourself, can you, Welles?"

"I love trouble," I flatly responded.

"Good," the guard spat. "You're gonna get plenty of it."

"Don't forget a room without a view," Malden said.

"That's right," the guard chuckled. "We'd best not forget the room without a view. Same one as last time, Welles?"

"Nuh-uh," Malden folded his arms. "That's too good for this murderer. Try the lower end of the spectrum."

"Would love to make his accommodations as miserable as possible, but all the other rooms are occupied."

"A shame we don't have a dungeon," Malden mused.

"Unfortunate, that," smirked the guard.

Back to clicking my heels in a cold interrogation room. Back to the door as thick as a phonebook slamming open with surly satisfaction. Back to the square-jawed man with short, white hair entering with a very unpleasant look, followed by Malden and Dixon. It felt like that Christmas Eve all over again.

"So, you're back to knocking people off, huh, Welles?" the square-jawed man snarled as he sat down.

"That's what they tell me."

"That's what they tell him," Dixon snorted. "As if the punk didn't know that he bumped his pal off."

"He knows it all," Malden snickered. "Don't you, Welles? You're a real smart guy. You think you're Shakespeare."

"Sure," the square-jawed man snarled. "Maybe even smart enough to know when to talk. Don't be shy, Welles. You can sing loud and plain. You're among friends."

"Let's have it, punk," Dixon jeered. "Are you gonna give it to us voluntarily, or are we gonna have to keep beating it out of you, punk?"

I smiled dreamily. "You say the cutest things."

"What'd you do it for?" the square-jawed man demanded.

"I didn't do anything."

"I'm not in the mood for jokes, twerp."

"Having me in here is a joke."

The square-jawed man leaned back and nodded. Dixon delivered another haymaker to my jaw.

"Go on, punk," Dixon spat. "*Talk*. You hear me, Welles? TALK."

"That's the punch line," the square-jawed man sneered. "Care for another?"

"I didn't kill Nigel."

"Then why did he call you twenty-two times right before he got rubbed?" the square-jawed man pursued. "And why did you answer a call for thirty-five seconds?"

"My phone kept ringing. I didn't recognize the number, but eventually I decided to answer. I figured it was a prank call."

"Who was on the other end?" the square-jawed man snapped.

"I didn't hear anything except a car's engine."

"What kind of car?" the square-jawed man narrowed his eyes.

"A 1947 Packard with no windshield wipers."

"Why should Wilfred want to call you?"

"He probably was in trouble."

"Oh, he was in trouble all right," Malden snorted around the toothpick. "You should know."

"You must be losing your touch, punk," Dixon sneered. "That isn't a very convincing story. Suppose you tell us a better one, punk."

"Quit stalling, Welles," the square-jawed man snorted. "How were you really mixed up with him and Bigelow?"

"Bigelow?"

"Whit Bigelow, not that you don't know," the square-jawed man said, with Malden and Dixon sneering in the background. "Owns a nightclub and art museum off Silver and Second called The Parthenon. Is president of an art exhibition called the Athena Society. A two-story building – nightclub on the first floor, society on the second floor. We've had dope on him for years that it's a front for a goods racket smuggling a bunch of Oriental junk. Wilfred was tied up with him somehow. Were you?"

"Oh, sure. I write novels by day and smuggle tapestries by night."

The Athena Society? The name slowly emerged from the back of my memory, like a vague dream you forget upon waking. Where had I heard it before?

"I remember you as sort of a noisy fella, Welles," the square-jawed man recalled as he scratched at his chin. "A guy that makes sound, and lots of it. The last time we had you in here, all you did was run that big mouth of yours. But now, all of a sudden, you get quiet."

"Tell us about Bigelow, punk," Dixon sneered, the maniacal delight he extracted from inflicting pain flaring up in his eyes. "Tell us what you and Wilfred were up to. Your pal get sick of the racket and decide to leave you with the bag? That why you bumped him off, punk?"

"Or," Malden smirked, "maybe he got sore at you and was gonna squeal to us about it. A guy in your position doesn't have any time for squealers, does he, Welles?"

"I didn't do it."

"Yeah, yeah, sure, sure," the square-jawed man sneered as he leaned forward. "We believe that like we believe in the tooth fairy."

"Tell us about Bigelow, punk," repeated Dixon.

"I don't know Bigelow, and I've never been to his place. How do you know Nigel was even involved with him? Bigelow tell you as much? Maybe he's lying. Maybe he killed Nigel."

"Well, well," the square-jawed man chuckled. "Welles wants to play cops and robbers. He's gonna solve his own crime. How about that, boys?"

"A crumb for all seasons," Malden smirked.

"The punk thinks he can do it all," Dixon said with a sardonic grin.

"You can't hold me without any evidence."

"Oh, yes, we can," the square-jawed man snarled. "We can hold anyone at any time for any reason, even if there isn't any evidence. You know why? Because we're *the law*. The law's never in the wrong, and it doesn't owe anyone an explanation for anything. Sure, there's no evidence tying you to Wilfred, but there's still evidence you're a smarmy punk we don't like. And if we can connect you to something, we're gonna do everything we can to connect you to something. We're gonna do everything we can to put scum like you where you belong. You're innocent? Tough. I'd rather see ninety-nine innocent jerks get the chair than see one guilty jerk go free."

"Cop justice, huh?" I said with disgust.

The square-jawed man glanced at the other two, then glared at me. He slammed his hands onto his knees and cocked his head at Malden.

"What do you say we *really* turn Dixon loose?"

"I say I like the sound of it," Malden smiled. Dixon's eyes twinkled sadistically.

Before he could proceed, a scrawny clerk poked his puny head into the room and mumbled something at the square-jawed man. He and Malden followed the guy into the corridor; a minute later, they came back inside. Malden leaned against the door, and the square-jawed man returned to the table. He rubbed at the same spot on his chin.

"Let him go," he grumbled.

"What?" Dixon shouted. "You can't just let him walk out of here. The punk's committed a crime. He deserves to *pay*."

"Sure he has, and sure he does," the square-jawed man assented, still glaring at me. "But his alibi checked out, and we don't have enough to keep him here."

Dixon spat, snorted, and stomped over. He uncuffed me with malice and gave me a sharp backhand for spite.

"You're lucky that's all you got, punk," he growled as he skulked away.

"You'd better watch your step, Welles," the square-jawed man said. "If I find one thing that even suggests you might be connected to anything with Wilfred, we'll grab your rear and throw it in the can where it belongs. And we won't let you go next time, not until they strap you in the chair and fry you 'till you're crisp as bacon."

Malden yanked open the door and Dixon sent me out with a final haymaker. I tumbled into the hall to a rowdy reception.

"Have a good time, runt?" a burly baldo in full uniform sneered as he stepped over me and plowed my stomach with his shoe.

"I don't think he's ready to go yet," a squat Mexican, also in full uniform, snickered. "What do you say, hooligan? You want another round of it?"

I staggered to my feet and stumbled out of there. The sun struck me like it was being filtered through a magnifying glass. The bright, blue sky looked savorless. The verdant trees looked sickly.

Not even the apotheosis of summer could lift my spirits; not even the middle of June could be cheerful. The world was a murk of cruel mystery.

4

IN A LONELY PLACE

Shelley's *Adonais* was top of mind, as the tumult of sadness swirled round me. Nigel paralleled John Keats – the subject of that poem – in that both perished before the promise of their youth could be fulfilled. I turned the first stanza of verse over in my head:

I weep for Adonais – he
is dead!

Oh, weep for Adonais!
though our tears

Thaw not the frost which binds so dear a head!

And thou, sad Hour, selected from all years

To mourn our loss, rouse thy obscure compeers,

And teach them thine own sorrow, say: "With me

Died Adonais; till the Future dares

Forget the Past, his fate and fame shall be

An echo and a light unto
eternity!

I wept bitterly. The eyes which always maintained a kindly spark were shut, ne'er again to open. The mind which always emitted the perfect balance of brilliance and imagination was empty, ne'er again to be filled. And the heart – oh, the heart! – that oft delighted to please another before itself was still, ne'er again to beat.

Confusion. Anguish. Grief. Remembrance. Mingled with my tears, these all blended together into a sorrowful brew that flooded the rest of that day and seeped into the next morning.

Nigel had many gifts, but he especially excelled at sketching and painting. He had gone to university to enhances these talents, to forge them into the tools by which he would conquer this realm and make man his servant.

Alas, the future was not so bright as it seemed it would be – a frequent phenomenon in this hollow world, where the best laid schemes o' mice an' men gang aft agley. Instead of rising to grandeur and glory by his abilities, my friend was dead. With rue, my heart was laden.

Why hadn't I done more to track him down? I always thought he had good reason for not saying where he was, and maybe he did, but that did not excuse my apathy in failing to find where he was. That did not excuse my ignoring his phone calls when he needed help. Regret hounded me inexorably.

Need a friend when you're in trouble? Need somebody to depend on when you're in a jam? Call Preston Welles, the novelist. He'll always leave you hanging. He'll always brush you off when you need him most. The more you do for him, the less he'll do for you.

But when grief had reduced to rumination, and tears had abated, and shock had subsided to the point I could begin to grasp the magnitude of it all, my mind moved away from mourning and toward suspicion.

Why had Nigel cut off contact with me and shared acquaintances? When and why had he come back to Albuquerque? Why was he reduced to running around with racketeers like Bigelow? And who was responsible for his demise?

I wanted to know it all. I had to know it all. And I wasn't going to sit idle while the law found somebody else to pin it on or clamped down with a cover up.

A brief public records search on his cousin Patty showed she lived off Bell Avenue and Edith Boulevard. The next morning, I would begin my investigation there.

As the daylight diminished and gave way to a dark night that mirrored my grief, I thought of Strauss' *Artist's Life.* Nigel and I often listened to it together, given its pertinence to the professions we intended to pursue. I turned it on.

While those familiar rhythms filled the air with a rueful ambiance, I reflected on the last time we had met – just before Christmas at an Uptown bakery.

It had been cold and cloudy all day. A strong, stiff wind whipped dead leaves across the frozen asphalt. Bare branches bent and shivered against the breeze. And although it was over forty degrees, the wind chill was in the twenties.

Eventually, I found a parking spot and lowered my head against the gale like Ebeneezer Scrooge trudging home on Christmas Eve. The sun stared powerlessly through a thin strip of clouds, like a flashlight trying to shine through a concrete wall.

Nigel was inside already, wearing a blue scarf, and light lapiz jeans, and a gray overcoat. His charcoal gloves were laid on the table, beside a cup of steaming hot chocolate, and his gold watch peeked its head out of his pocket.

"If I didn't know any better," Nigel grinned as I shook his hand strongly, "I'd say you were cold. Where'd you park?"

"About a mile north. Santy Claus had to lend me his sleigh."

"Not you. You only get lumps of coal."

"I do?"

"Authors are notorious delinquents. They're always getting into trouble."

"Is that so?"

"That's so. Why, I even heard about one fellow who was accused of killing three different people. He had to hide out at a friend's cottage for a month in between two of the slayings."

"You left out the part about his being innocent."

"That's right," he snapped his fingers. "How careless of me. And I haven't even bothered to tell you how satisfied I am to hear of the success of your book, have I, Welles? I always predicted you were going to be more famous than I. You have too much talent to be anything but eminent, renowned, distinguished, august."

"Don't be premature in prophecy," I replied. "You'll have to wait until your paintings are displayed before you can say that for certain."

"*If* my paintings are displayed," he muttered.

Nigel took out his watch, as he was wont to do, and opened it so it played a music box melody of the last thirty-five seconds of the fourth waltz in *Artist's Life*. He turned it over in his hand as I'd seen him do since he was a boy, then slipped it back into his pocket. A brooding expression flashed across his face.

I intended to parse the matter further, but the waiter came. By the time we had given our orders, Nigel's usual vigor and warmth had returned.

It was a charming little bakery. Warm orange lanterns dangled above each table, throwing a festive, friendly light around the room. The white walls were covered with chalkboard menus and simple sketches of pastries. Wreaths and Christmas lights adorned the glass counters, and a small, artificial Christmas tree stood in the corner opposite them.

The counters were full of delectable things – donuts that dripped with glaze, muffins as big as mole hills, scones drizzled with sugar, cookies that crumbled into salivating chunks, cupcakes covered with icing, cakes as wide as computer monitors. Atop one counter was a small radio that played an orchestral version of "O Come All Ye Faithful."

"How's the university life, Nigel?" I asked.

"The university life? Splendid. A venerable institution, Dartmouth. Beautiful buildings. Idyllic country. Timeworn soil. Welles, you won't know wonder until you have before you the New England countryside on a warm autumn day. There's a nook by the Connecticut River – a tranquil, shady spot beneath the sycamore, with a seat of grass, and the gentle flowing of the water – about which a man of your talents could write a book of verse with ease."

"I'll consider it."

"I've sat there many afternoons, Welles. I've thought, like Wordsworth, of the still, sad music of humanity, and contrasted it with the mirthful melodies of the meadow. But I have no reason to lament what man has made of man. Have the world; give me only that blissful nook, and let me dream my time away."

"Sounds like a swell spot, Nigel," I remarked as I glanced out the window behind me. The clouds remained, but the sun was starting to spread its rays across the sky.

"I wouldn't have thought it so beautiful in my dreams. After I graduate, I intend to stay near the river in a charming cottage that would make for a perfect studio. Inspiration is never far from man in scenes as those."

"What have you made lately?"

"A watercolor of the river with the sun dipping into a row of copses," Nigel replied with much satisfaction, following a sip. "Then, a sketch of a meadow in fog after heavy snow. It was a bit more demanding than the watercolor, but I welcomed the challenge."

"Send me pictures of them. You haven't shown me any of your work since your painting of the hillside near campus."

"That is my favorite, so far. I have hopes the Athena Society will accept it, but they diminish by the day."

"The Athena Society?"

"An internationally acclaimed art museum downtown. I would catapult to fame and fortune, if ever its owner accepted one of my pictures. But I don't think he will."

"Why not?"

"Why does anyone reject art? He does not like it, I suppose. That's why..."

"Why what?"

"No matter, Welles."

I wondered at his pause, especially when the brooding expression returned to his face. But he wouldn't say anything more on the matter.

"Do you ever paint people?" I asked after a few minutes.

"I did a full portrait of one of my professors, Mr. Enders. Hair is one of the most difficult objects for me to paint properly, but that wasn't an issue here because he hasn't any. And there was Mrs. Kemsingworth, the lady who lives near the cottage I desire. I gave it to her when she turned one hundred."

"Any girls?"

"None, aside from Mrs. Kemsingworth, but I confess to have interest in courting one in particular."

"Oh?"

"The most splendid girl in the world, Welles. I'm sorry I had to cancel our dinner the other night, but she detained me longer than I expected, and I submitted to her company with pleasure."

"Submitting to a dame's company with pleasure? When girls followed you around in school, you were indifferent, if not oblivious. How you've changed, Nigel!"

"I suppose I have. But there is something about her that none of the others had. Something beyond the usual feminine charm. Something that, that, well, I can't particularly describe it. Someday, you'll see it for yourself."

We had turnovers and talked of Hogarth's paintings and Lord Byron's poetry and Strauss' waltzes and our boyhood memories and the people and places and things that colored them.

Then, we shook hands like we always did, agreed to see each other again soon, and parted. I didn't think it would be the last time, not as he strolled away with his usual gait, his hair blowing smoothly in the wind, his mind pondering his next endeavor.

The memory evaporated. That was where I had heard the Athena Society mentioned before. Nigel wanted Bigelow to display his paintings, naturally. But did Bigelow want something in return? And who was this girl that mesmerized him as no girl had before?

5

THE MODERN IMBECILE

During the night, while I tossed and turned from vague dreams of Nigel, his grandfather's birthday celebration two years ago vividly came to mind. His grandparents had lived in an enormous estate off San Rafael Avenue just west of Tramway Boulevard, somewhat near the famed Nichols family.

A golden summer sun flowed placidly through the gentle panes of the old house's expansive library. Nigel, engrossed in Aristotle, leaned in an armchair; I lounged on a davenport and watched the afternoon shadows creep across the marble floor. I would pick a book myself once the shadows reached a bust of Tennyson on one of the bookshelves.

Nigel closed Aristotle and ran a hand across his eyes.

"How did the ancients find time to live, Welles?" he asked me after a yawn. "I devote every waking moment to study and sketching, yet I remain sorely in want of wisdom. They lived full lives and learned more difficult subjects faster than I do."

"I don't think they did," I answered, "though they were far superior to modern man."

"Modern man is the fool Livy rebuked for being unable to tolerate neither his own vices nor their remedies. He conceives farcical systems of governance, and cheap, commodified culture which pale in comparison to kingdoms past, yet has the audacity to think himself enlightened and superior to previous generations. My next sketch will portray the folly of this present world. I intend to call it *The Modern Imbecile*."

"That's what you should call yourself," a voice that befitted a pubescent teenage boy snarled, and Patty tramped into the room. Even for an occasion as this, she couldn't bother to dress better than black pajamas and bathroom slippers. Her oily, blonde hair was tied up in a taut bun.

"Here's your subject, Nigel," I said.

"Don't waste your energy acknowledging her, Welles. She only comes to these events to make life difficult on honorable persons as ourselves."

"Partly, and partly to remind the old bird I've got as much a right to some of his dough as you do," Patty spat. "Maybe I haven't been getting much of it lately. Maybe he got an idea to keep it all to hisself, except what he gives you to waste with your crayons."

"My art is my purpose for existence," Nigel said steadfastly. "Once I have no more to share with mankind, I should wish to perish, rather than toil in drudgery all my days."

"Go on and get it over with, then," Patty snorted. "Maybe I'd get some of that dough I deserve while I could enjoy using it."

"Welles," Nigel continued, as if the tramp wasn't even in the library, "I would give my very soul if it would but ensure the immortality of my art. I would sacrifice my body to the devouring beak of the eagle, like Prometheus, if it would but grant to humanity the heavenly works I wish to produce. I would submit to heaving the stone up the hill, like Sisyphus, should my art obtain the sanction of the gods."

"You'll be famous, Nigel. You're too gifted to be otherwise."

"Ah, but many a gifted artist labors unappreciated, Welles! How many geniuses of ages past were unknown in their time, or, what's worse, ridiculed and reviled, and only received due recognition long after they shuffled off this mortal coil? No, that must not be my fate. It cannot be my fate. I should bring upon myself the rack, and submit to be drawn and quartered, if thereby my art will be honored while I am but a blooming youth."

"The rack's too good for you," Patty snarled before trundling to the door. Then, she paused and spun around with a grotesque sneer. "Oh yeah, that old bird wanted me to have you and Welles come down before the guests left. Guess I didn't tell you until after they left. Guess I must have forgotten."

I slammed the heavy door in her hideous face and went back to the davenport.

"Why do you put up with that worthless slug?"

"Because I pity her, in spite of herself," was Nigel's considered reply. "I used to despise her until I realized it is she who suffers by her despicable nature, and not myself. But the topic merits no further consideration. As I read Aristotle, you were thinking deep thoughts and watching light move across the room. Shall we make conversation of the two subjects?"

"Naturally," I smiled.

The memory faded as quickly as it had appeared, and I was left with the silent stillness of the night.

I was washing my face the next morning when loud knocking leaped into the bathroom. The cops may have come back, but they weren't coming back in. Not unless they broke down my door and let the bullets fly, as they're so prone to do.

"Preston Welles?" squeaked a flimsy voice that wouldn't belong to any cop. A slender man, about forty, in an absurdly fitted black sportscoat, preposterously thin black pants that stopped at his calves, and an orange necktie that reached his thighs kept on knocking with his right hand and holding a brown attache with his left hand. He looked like a scarecrow.

"Preston Welles?" the scarecrow repeated when I opened the door.

"Uh-huh. What's on your mind?"

"Well, uh, I came here, actually, to find out what's on your mind. Preston Welles, the government is concerned about your, about your wellbeing."

The scarecrow fumbled through the attache until he presented a rectangular white card that was sharp enough to score steaks. The card read: *Tyler J. Amthor, Psychiatric Consultant.*

"My wellbeing, huh?"

"Yes. They have conducted an extensive campaign to send representatives of the American Psychiatric Counsel door to door in every city in the country. The government is concerned about undiagnosed mental health issues going unreported and, and, uh, leading to unnecessary distress and confusion. When was your most recent mental health evaluation?"

"Never." I poked the card that could score steaks against the door frame. The corners didn't bend.

"That, that isn't ideal. Uh, suppose we sat down for a few minutes and talked over some of your options. It's very important to receive mental health treatment on a regular basis, that is, if it's necessary, which seems like it would be necessary in your case."

"Why's that?" I asked coldly.

"Uh, well, it may not be necessary, actually," Amthor simpered. "But, but, since you haven't been seen by an expert, it's difficult to tell. Suppose we sat down for a few minutes and talked over some of your options. You might, uh, you might find the exercise very refreshing."

"Might I?" I twirled the card. It made me think of a batarang.

"Certainly possible. Why, I was just speaking to the aged woman down the street from you, and she was very surprised to learn she possibly had several minor behavioral disorders. Anyone could have them. Could have behavioral disorders, I mean. Suppose we sat down for a few minutes and talked over some of your options."

"All right," I flicked the card back at him. "Start talking."

"Uh, this isn't a very private place to do it. Suppose we..."

"Suppose you go away."

I shut the door. The scarecrow stood on my porch for a minute, putting his hands on his hips like he didn't know how to put his hands on his hips, then sauntered to the next house. He walked like he had three legs.

I was getting into my car, a 2003 Mazda Protege, to head to Patty's when the scarecrow emerged from across the street.

"Preston Welles!" he gasped while waving a cream-colored card in his hand. "Wait!"

I leaned against the driver's door as Amthor staggered up my driveway and pushed his hands against his kneecaps to catch his breath. Then, I plucked the card out of his paw. *Chandler Murdoch, Transpersonal Psychiatry* was centered in a faint Oriental font, with a phone number and a website and an address in the Spruce Park neighborhood spread across the bottom.

"Like this Murdoch, huh?"

"Murdoch? Why, why, yes, he is absolutely one of the finest psychiatrists in the country, if not the world," the scarecrow smiled like somebody was pinching his ear. "Murdoch is, is an outstanding pupil of the human mind and soul. Have you heard of him?"

"No."

"Oh, that is to your detriment, Preston Welles. You must make an appointment to see him immediately, even if you don't believe you have any mental health conditions. His brilliance will make, will make you so much better than you thought you were. Should I ask him to schedule an appointment for you? He may have openings soon. You could be seeing him by the end of the week, possibly. And, and then perhaps that would unleash some of the hatred and anger within you."

"I'll unleash some of it on you if you don't leave me alone."

The scarecrow emitted a nervous squeak, like a mouse cornered by a tomcat, then closed his attache and loosened the tie that reached his thighs and motored off walking like he had three legs. The card went to my pocket because I had a strange urge not to throw it away.

Patty's house had seen better days. Cracked, crumbling beige stucco framed greasy glass panes that looked like they would shatter if you stared at them too hard. Deformed shingles that had blown off the roof years ago served as thrifty decorations for a barren dirt lot sparsely populated by dead weeds.

A filthy, plastic, powder blue chair was on the porch, and a faded, plastic Santa Claus was standing by the door, holding a bag of gifts with both hands. He looked like he had been holding the bag for a long time and was about to collapse from exhaustion. I tapped him on the shoulder for encouragement.

A man in his late thirties answered the door. His idea of a haircut was completely shaved sides and a clump of black hair set like a perm in the front and a mullet in the back. His idea of fashion was a black, sleeveless shirt of a bald boxer's face and baggy, black shorts that reached his crumb-sized calves. And his idea of fitness was a gut which bulged the shirt forward, like he was pregnant. I doubted he could bench press a broomstick.

"What do you want?" he snapped and scratched at his scraggly beard and folded his scrawny arms. His voice had the intonation of a dying duck emitting its final breaths in agony.

"Patty. She lives in this hovel, doesn't she?"

"Who's asking?"

"I am. Do I go in there, or does she come out here?"

"Who is it, Carlos?" Patty growled from inside.

"Some creep asking for you."

"Tell him I'm busy."

"Did you hear that?" Carlos asked smugly. "She's busy."

I brushed him aside and entered a dingy hallway that quickly opened up to a small living room and a smaller kitchen.

What a foul place. The ceiling was too low, the windows were too dirty, and the air was too thick. Where regular people hung pictures and displayed vases, there were filthy smears and dirty socks. Where human beings ate dinner and watched television, these pigs piled unwashed underwear and plates of half-eaten food. This whole putrid property reeked of inhumanity and hate.

The only furniture in the living room was a coffee table supporting a small TV and a soiled couch on which Patty was sprawled, tapping furiously at a phone game. She was wearing a sleeveless, stained top and stained pajama pants with sickly polka dots that complemented the lazy bun that was sliding down her head. Same old Patty.

"So, it's Preston Welles," she croaked. "Same sharp character, only your clothes are fresher and you've filled out. What'd you come by for? You want me to congratulate you on being famous? Well, I won't. You just heard about Nigel, and you come crawling by to offer your sympathies, ain't you?"

"When'd you see him last?"

"What do you care?"

The used matches which covered the floor crunched under my feet as I went to the window facing the "back yard" and watched a scrawny cat groom itself with smugness.

"You killed him for the dough."

"For the dough, huh?" Patty snorted. "I ain't opposed to knocking off an artsy snob like that, especially if I'd get dough for doing it. But I ain't get no dough, Welles. You know why? 'Cause the old bird cut me out of the will. Left all his property and dough to Nigel's uncle, who don't even live in this country. I didn't get a penny."

"Sorry to hear that, sweetheart," I sneered.

"This guy's a cop, babe," Carlos told Patty. "He's trying to pin something on us."

"Nice try, brainiac, but I'm here on other interests."

"Sure," Patty smirked. "He didn't come by to give me no condolences; he's here for the publicity. Probably going to post on social media about it and then he'll tell the news he was here. The headlines will say, 'Noble Welles visits grieving cousin of close friend'."

"Welles, huh?" Carlos spat. "I don't like that name. It makes me angry."

"An IQ above twenty would make you angry," I snorted.

"Did you shed big, bubbly tears when you find out, Welles?" Patty sneered. "Did you get real sad when you learned what became of your great pal? Don't expect me to be interested in setting up no funeral. For all I care, that dope could be buried at sea."

"Shut up, you slimy tramp," I snarled through my teeth. Somehow, she had managed to become even more despicable than she always had been.

Carlos stepped between us with arms akimbo, then marched within a gnat's wingspan of me.

“Don’t be coming in my house and insulting my girl like that, punk,” he sniveled.

“Calling this place a house is hyperbole.”

“What’d you say? What word did you use?”

“Hyperbole.”

“Yeah. What kind of racist doubletalk is that?”

“Try using a dictionary. You know what those are, don’t you?”

“Your name’s making me angry. You’re making me angry. You keep making me angry, and I’ll make you feel pain.”

“You couldn’t make a moth feel pain.”

“Get out of the way, Carlos,” Patty grumbled; he sullenly retreated.

“How long had Nigel been back in town?” I asked.

“Pfff. How should I know?”

“Where’d he live? Where’d he work?”

“Might have mentioned a nightclub for rich jerks that he wanted to show off that trash he painted. Might have mentioned a boarding house off Edith and Gold. But I ain't know much else, so quit acting like me and him was close, Welles. That punk never meant nothing to me.”

“Don’t call him that, you worthless slug.”

In the window’s filthy reflection, I saw Carlos heave a Bose speaker at my head. When I sidestepped it, he tried four times more. Persistent, for a twig. I pummeled him until he staggered and smacked him over the couch.

All the while, Patty had been observing the beatdown with contemptible wonder and depraved delight. She only moved to light a cigarette and flip the match to the floor.

“Who was Nigel running around with?” I asked. “Nobody else knew he was back in town. Why’d he leave us all in the dark?”

“You ask a lot for free, ain't you, Welles?” Patty spat as Carlos crawled along the adjacent wall like a wingless fly. "Give me five hundred, and we can have a nice chat about your punk pal. I can tell you all the different ways I hated his guts. That sounds like a good proposition to me. What do you say? Are you gonna give me five hundred?”

“I wouldn’t give you the string off a banana.”

She threw her ugly head back, cranked open her hideous mouth, and gargled a disgusting cackle. The odious swine.

6

THE BOARDING HOUSE

I stood looking up at a two-story building of bright red brick and heavy wooden shutters and a surmounted weathercock atop a small cupola. Small trees and small hedges occupied the space between the sidewalk and the house, and a bronze knocker that looked older than the Magna Carta protruded from the door.

An old black lady with tiny eyeglasses jerked the door open and eyed me suspiciously.

"I'm Preston Welles, ma'am. You had a boarder named Nigel Wilfred."

"Mm-hm."

"Could I ask you some questions about him? He was my friend."

"Your friend?" she scowled. "If he was your friend, then how come I ain't never seen you with him or hear him say yo name before?"

I expected her to be suspicious, so I produced a photo of me and Nigel at the bakery that final time. The old lady looked down at the photo, then up at me, then down at the photo again.

"What was his favorite color?" she asked.

"Turquoise."

"How 'bout his favorite actor?"

"Humphrey Bogart."

She looked down at the picture, then handed it to me and broke off a toothy grin.

"Ain't nobody would know that about Nigel, 'cept for his friends," she bellowed. "Come on in, honey child."

I followed her into a fine foyer with an old grandfather clock opposite a homely armchair. The faint murmur of old jazz I had heard outside grew louder as we approached the kitchen, where a small radio sat on a circular table.

"Sit down, Preston," the old lady gestured at a chair and hummed the tune. "That's George Lewis playing, that is. It done make my soul shout fo' joy. Only thing better's good company. I like having good company, ever since Wilbur... But Nigel and I was always chopping up. Ain't never got along with a boarder so well."

"How long had Nigel been staying here, ma'am?"

"Five months, about. Come in one day asking for a room. I sees he's a nice young man and got work at a diner, I says sure. Always pay his bill on time, Nigel does. Always got a nice word fo' the old lady, even if there ain't no reason fo' any. One night, he ain't get back till past two, and I figures I sit up fo' him, see if he's hiding something. He walk through that door and see me setting there waiting for him, and he jest gets to laughing. 'Mrs. Hattie', he say – my name's Hattie – 'Mrs. Hattie, you ain't gotta sit there all night like I was yo son. I ain't in no trouble. You go on and gets you rest.' I says, 'Nigel, I just checking up on you, making show you ain't running round wit no shady guys.' He say, 'Aw, no, Mrs. Hattie, I ain't got nothing to do wit shady. I just been getting to know my lady a little better.' And from then on, I know he ain't a boy to hide nothing."

"Do you remember the diner's name?"

"The diner? No, I ain't remember Nigel never telling me the name, only he always left wearing his uniform, and I figures it must've been near by cause he ain't got a car."

If Nigel didn't have a car, whose car was he driving when he died?

"He ever bring anybody in here?"

"Brought a freckly fella that played on the same ball team as him. But not often. Only other time I seen him with anybody was when his lady picks him up one afternoon. I's weeding my lawns when this car pull up and she git out to ask for him. Ho, ho, cute as a June bug, she was. Ain't ever hear her name, but, Lord have mercy, honey, was she pretty."

"How was he acting the last few days, Mrs. Hattie? Was he worried about anything?"

"He show was, honey child. Day he met the good Lord, he ain't hardly say a word. Told me before he go out he ain't comin' back early cause they needed extra work at the diner, and there ain't more to tell."

I leaned back in the soft chair and watched the sunlight stream through the blinds. The radio kept pumping out those tunes, and she kept humming to them.

"Did anything look like it was missing from his room?"

"Truth is, I ain't had the heart to go in there since it happened. Morning after, I open the door and look in and I ain't take no mo'. Don't feel right. Don't look right, not having him coming and going. Any of my other boarders go like that make me a sad old lady. But Nigel go like that make me a sad, sad, sad, sad, sad old lady. Bright young man going off and getting killed. Mm."

"Do you suspect anyone?"

"Naw, but I ain't got no reason to. Besides, ain't never can tell who a man's enemies is."

"Do you mind if I look around his room?"

"Heavens no, I don't mind," Hattie reached into a pocket of her dress and handed me the key. "Take all the time you need. I gots these biscuits to bake. Have a few with me when they's ready, won't you?"

"I'd be delighted to," I smiled.

The stairs were carpeted and quiet. Nigel's room was the fifth door from the left in a warm hall covered by a long rug that an elephant could walk on without making a sound.

It was all familiar – the busts of Hogarth and Apelles, the statuette of Raphael, Nigel's paintings alongside those of Suffolk and Constable, the easel he had employed since we were boys. I hadn't anticipated feeling much emotion from seeing the room, because I knew Nigel had all of these things, and could guess how he would arrange them. But one look at them was all it took to draw more sorrow from my soul. Truly did Tennyson write in *Enoch Arden*, "things seen are mightier than things heard."

Eventually, I got up from the floor where my crestfallen state had compelled me to sink. Further reminiscence could wait. For now, I needed clues that would point me to what he had been up to and who did this to him. My resolve was as solid as concrete.

In Nigel's closet, I found a Zhongshan suit that belied his tastes, and a baseball jersey which read "Watermelons" on the front and "Wilfred" on the back. His drawers were disheveled and things on a small desk appeared out of place. Somebody had been in here - maybe the somebody who knocked him off. Could it have been Whit Bigelow?

I'd one foot out the door when I noticed the pocket watch sitting solemnly on the dresser. I turned it over in my hand as Nigel had so often done and listened tearfully to its tune. Then, I slipped it into my pocket, gave the room another glance, and shut the door on the last abode that had belonged to my friend.

Hattie was pulling a rack of enormous biscuits out of the oven when I returned to the kitchen. The radio was still pumping out those tunes, and she was still humming to them.

"You's jest in time, honey child. I ain't letting you out this room 'till you gits you a few."

According to Hattie's numerology, "a few" meant nine, and only after they had been loaded down with a stick of butter each. While I gorged myself, I obtained her permission for the pocket watch and learned she hadn't seen anybody different come by after Nigel's demise. Whoever went through his room had a key.

On my way home, I started to wonder what the law was telling their pals in the press to say about Nigel's death, so I stopped at a gas station and bought a copy of the *Albuquerque Tribune*. I hadn't read this rag since M.K. Matthewson had been chucked out his office window, but it looked as duplicitous as ever.

The front page featured the usual insipid tripe playing up the false left-right paradigm, and proclaiming the sacredness of the racket called "democracy", and hawking the latest technocrat enslavement trends as beneficial to mankind, and bemoaning the want of "professionalism" amongst puppet politicians as they performed their phony conflicts and scripted feuds.

I snorted, then started when I saw an unflattering photo of myself beneath the headline, "WELLES SUSPECTED OF SLAYING FRIEND." The article was written by W. Randolph Dexter, Matthewson's longtime colleague:

"Preston Welles – the novelist whose rise to eminence has been sullied by suspicions of bigotry and violence – was arrested yesterday afternoon on suspicion of murdering Nigel Wilfred, his close friend. That Welles would slay one so dear to him seems unsurprising, given the intolerance and impropriety which our sterling late colleague, M. K. Matthewson, proved to personify Welles' character and conduct. We should not soon forget those outstanding reports skewering Welles' odious nature – outstanding reports which led to Welles physically assaulting M.K. before dozens of witnesses at a ball and then being connected to his unfortunate passing. To say that Welles is a truly reprehensible human being is merely to acknowledge and proclaim the truth, which is our sole objective here at the *Tribune*.

"Alas, it appears Welles has once more managed to foil justice, if but for the time being. According to sources familiar with the situation, but who are not authorized to speak publicly, Welles was released from custody after the police were unable to determine that his alibi was false, in spite of much incriminating evidence. While our public servants at the police department tirelessly labor to obtain sufficient evidence that will enable them to apprehend Welles, they have ruled Wilfred's death was the result of his arrogant attempts to show off while driving at high speed. When Wilfred lost control of the vehicle, the impact of the crash charred both himself and the car."

I angrily flipped through the rest of the paper, which had another article on Nigel's burgeoning art career and reinforced the lie that his "recklessness" had led to his death. Unsurprisingly, no mention was made of his being sapped.

Much as the lies about myself in that article infuriated me, and much as I wanted to take a poke at this rat who replaced Matthewson, more important was what the article was implying. Since the law figured they couldn't hang a murder rap on me, they told their presstitute pals to publish a despicable, racy myth that shallow minds always gravitate towards – a sordid bundle of lies that claimed Nigel died by his own folly, rather than by the malice of another.

So much for those flatfoots wanting to know what Bigelow had to do with anything. They were covering it up on Bigelow's behalf.

But why should I expect anything different? The law and the press have long been partners in covering up for the people that control them. Somebody with clout must have wanted Nigel's real cause of death hidden from the obtuse public eye. But why?

When I got home, I found a Facebook page for the Watermelons. They would practice this afternoon at five at a high school field near Candelaria Road and Pennsylvania Street.

Nostalgia from my Little League days built as I walked from the parking lot to the field, the sights and sounds of my boyhood returning to me after many years, the thought of Nigel in all those bygone scenes.

A guy in the dugout was watching me reminisce. A short, pudgy guy with rectangular, thick-rimmed glasses with lenses as big as iPhones and wrinkled brown hair that didn't look or smell like he washed it very often. What hair wasn't crammed beneath a soiled baseball cap with a logo of a snarling duck wearing a hood had crusted as it curled above the neck. He complemented this headpiece with an oversized, milk white t-shirt with a logo of a brawny beaver growling and grappling with an enormous baseball, and preposterously flabby gray baseball pants about eight inches too long.

"Where's your hat?" the gnome demanded nasally, displaying a jagged stable of banana-colored fangs that smelled like Roquefort cheese.

"I didn't bring one."

"You *didn't bring one*? Why not? Don't you know ball players always wear hats? You can't play without a hat. And it better not be a Dodger hat. All they do is choke and ruin baseball."

"I'm not here to play, Igor," I informed him as I squeezed past – a difficult feat, given the narrow dugout and the hefty blob which congested it – and stepped onto an uneven dirt infield.

"Oh yeah you are. Nobody comes to a ballfield unless it's to play ball. Ball players only wear spikes. You're wearing tennis shoes. We're not playing tennis, bub, we're playing baseball out here. Got that?"

"Whatever you say, pal."

By the backstop was a sour looking sexagenarian – the same one I had seen online called the Watermelons' manager, Earl Fuller – wearing a maroon varsity jacket and gray baseball pants that stopped at the shins. He scowled and stuffed his hands beneath his armpits.

"Where's your hat? If you're a ball player, you've gotta have a hat. Nobody ever played ball without a hat. You're a disgrace to baseball and a danger to the rest of us without a hat. And you better not bring any Dodger hats out here. I won't associate with anyone who supports a team of chokers that are bad for baseball."

"Nigel Wilfred used to play for you, didn't he?"

"Wilfred? Why? What do you need to know for?"

"I'm trying to find out what happened to him."

"What happened to him? What's the matter with you? Don't you follow the news? He burned up because of his vanity and arrogance. He was trying to get cute and it cost him big time. But that's always what happens whenever these young punks try to show off. They think they're cool. Why, back when I was your age, I had..."

Fuller gasped when I seized his collar. Fear crept across his steely gray eyes.

"Nigel had a friend on your team with red hair and freckles, didn't he?"

"Uh, you, you mean Fitch? Fitch and Wilfred were pals."

"Is he still on your team?"

"Yeah, sure, he's still on my team. Why, why there he is right now."

Approaching us was a slender, freckle-faced man about my age with fluffy hair as red as Smaug.

"This jerk that won't wear a hat wants to talk to you, Fitch," Fuller snorted as he shoved his hands back underneath his armpits and stomped away.

"My name's Welles. Nigel Wilfred was my friend."

"I liked him," Fitch squeaked, extending a clammy, floppy right hand that seemed to shrink as I shook it.

"I'm trying to find out what really happened to him. Could I talk to you after practice?"

"No time for that," Fitch shook his head and twirled a frizzy hair between his left thumb and pointer finger. "I got practice."

"Practice?"

"Trumpet practice. I'm in a 40s swing band. Strictly throwback, see. None of the modern stuff. Like the racket?"

"Hate the racket."

"Play the piano?"

"Play the piano."

"Hate the racket, play the piano. Shame. We've been looking for a pianist ever since Nigel..."

"Nigel was in your band?"

"Sure. Preferred the classical stuff, but he adapted fast. Made it sound like he played swing all his life."

Other members of the group knew Nigel, and they might know things about him that Fitch didn't. Much as I disliked jazz, I didn't want to pass this opportunity up.

"I'd like to talk to your whole group about him."

"Fine by me," Fitch shrugged.

Through the rest of the practice I tried to extract information from Nigel's former teammates, but Fitch was the only one who knew anything about him. That was Nigel. He only made himself known to kindred spirits.

While I waited, memory once more appeared before me. During the springtime last year, I was having dinner with Bucy, Peter McClain, and Nigel. It was his first appearance since my first novel had been published.

"Congratulations, Welles," Bucy smiled as he looked over a copy. "Keep learning and improving, and you'll be up there with the best of them."

"Thanks to you I will," I nodded deferentially. "If you hadn't read my manuscript, none of this would have happened."

"It astounds me, Welles," Nigel said, "how eighteen publishing houses could reject your manuscript. Are they all really that imbecilic?"

"Sure, they are," I snorted, still smarting from the sardonic e-mail by which the Burqueno Publishing House had scoffed at my story. "Remember what Carson used to say about publishing houses, Bucy?"

"Of course," Bucy replied. "Good old Carson – a charming guy that got infatuated with the wrong girl. You know, you owe as much to him as you to do me, Welles, because if he had never hired you, I'd have never known about your story. Come with me the next time I visit him. He's as spry as a guy that's in a cage all day can be."

A familiar rolling voice came from the doorway. Peter was wearing a purple bow tie and a white flannel shirt beneath a silver coat. His black shoes were polished and his socks were silver.

"Man marks the earth with ruin," he declared despondently as he twirled his walking stick. "His control stops with the shore, for who can dwell upon the face of the deep but the beasts to which it is beholden?"

"Your stick, sir," said a waiter expecting him to check his garments.

"This is not a stick, fondly stripling," Peter scoffed while stamping the stick. "It is a sceptre like that of Zeus, by which I command all mortals and gods from the heavenly mount. It is a staff like that of Merlin, by which the fiends of Camelot are foiled. Do you not know the McClain coat of arms, witless wight? You do not? Alas, authority forgets a dying king. Obedience is the bond of rule, and if the liege is clouded by his own conceit, what becometh of the kingdom?"

"Your stick, sir," the waiter repeated meekly.

"The audacity of your impertinence will be known throughout the kingdom," Peter replied, "for I shall command my knights to hang you from yonder tree as a warning to all who would defile their sovereign."

The waiter tremblingly bowed his head, and Peter took his place at the table.

"Welles," said he, "your talent bespeaks genius, but your genius bewrayeth not your talent. I adored your book; I am ravished with your idea for a second. What shall I be with your third, and fourth, and beyond?"

"Maybe you'll marry them," I snorted.

"Marry them?" Peter frowned as he opened a wine bottle with alacrity. "No, that isn't advisable. There are laws in this state respecting polygamy. Besides, if I were to marry your books, what ever should become of my dear lady?"

"*You* have a dear lady?" Bucy asked.

"Certainly, I do. Have I not exhibited the verse by which I extol her virtues?" Peter reached into his breast pocket and retrieved a carefully folded paper.

"If it's anything like your other poems," I said, "we can do without it."

"Ah, Welles, you disclose your weakness," Peter shook his head as he tucked the paper away. "You excel at prose, but shrink from poetry. These things ought not so be. Should not the artist delight in all genres?"

"Welles delights in his novels, McClain," Nigel said, "and profits thoroughly thereby."

"And so he does," Peter said, after a long sip. "But to see him at an event as this, and no fair maiden at his elbow? No, that will not do. Marriage is honorable in all, Welles. You charm young ladies by your novels as Orpheus charmed man and beast by his melodies. There is no excuse for having not brought one here."

Nigel took a pad and began to sketch furiously. He was drawing Aphrodite upon a gilded throne, with her votaries teeming before her.

"Very fine, Nigel," I said when he had laid his pencil down and was looking over the sheet with satisfaction.

"Thank you, Welles," he replied. "It's the kind of girl I seek for myself – one that will bolster me in ways I could never dream of bolstering myself. An Aphrodite in human flesh to accompany me all my days. I have never seen the girl I draw, but I know she exists, and the day I meet her will be the day I ascend to heights unforeseen. The commonplace woman does no benefit to my art; I rather find she impedes me. But this damsel whom I desire, she shall inspire me in ways no other maiden will or can inspire me. I will go to the ends of the earth with her."

Nigel passed his sketch around the table as he spoke.

"Cold Pastoral!" Peter declared. "When old age shall this generation waste, thou shalt remain, in midst of other woe than ours, a friend to man, to whom thou say'st, 'Beauty is truth, truth beauty', - that is all ye know on earth, and all ye need to know."

"Any candidates for the role?" I asked.

"Not at the moment," said Nigel.

"Beware of rich English blondes with crusty old fathers. And butlers like Dracula and houses like Buckingham Palace. Those types tend to be maniacs."

"So I heard," he smiled.

The girl that had come by the boarding house, and of whom Nigel had spoken so glowingly, must have mirrored this sketch.

I intended to find out who she was and what she knew about what led to his demise.

7

NIGHT AND THE CITY

Sure, I disliked jazz. I didn't understand how anyone could listen to it without tearing their ears off in agony. But there were greater things at stake than music tastes. Fitch might have handed me a meal ticket to tracking down who knocked off Nigel, and I wasn't about to throw it away just because I couldn't stand the soundtrack.

The practice studio was a dingy, downtown hole in the wall off Copper Avenue and Fifth Street. Evidently, Fitch's group had started without him, because as we were walking down a dismal, windowless, concrete hall, the first few of those sly notes slid through the air and into my ears. When Fitch caught wind of the rhythms, he began to twitch and twist and shake, like they were his master and he was their servant.

He flipped open a metal door and the sound poured out like a tidal wave. The hall may have been cold, but the hole in the wall was hot, red hot, sweltering with the heat of passion and the furnace of sound. Five other guys were in the room, each playing their instruments with incontinent abandon. Fitch shimmied over to a set of drums, grabbed the sticks, and joined in on the act.

What a racket of noise. I wouldn't call it music – just noise, roaring noise, deafening noise, the kind of noise that could bring down walls and set off earthquakes and start revolutions. It all coalesced into a cacophony of discordant notes, twisted rhythms, rambunctious tunes.

Oh, did they play. They pumped and pounded and shook and swung and shrieked, exuded volumes of sweat and heart and soul. Yes, noise – noise of maniacal melodies, crackling concertos, screaming symphonies, seasoned with grit and guts and grunts.

I couldn't say how long it went on. Maybe it was a few minutes; maybe it was a few hours. But a strange sensation came over me, the longer I listened to the confusion – a sensation that bewitched me to drop my misgivings against everything base and vile and indulge whatever foul ideas came to mind. Before I could act on this beastly impulse, the practice ended, and the performers came up for air.

"This the new pianist, Fitch?" asked the trombonist, a guy in his early thirties with crimson cheeks and a substantial stomach.

"He's a pianist, Jigger, but not the new one," Fitch huffed and puffed. "He doesn't like the racket."

"Took it pretty well just now," opined a scrawny clarinetist.

"He don't like it, Character," Fitch told him.

"This guy a badge, Fitch?" the trumpeter asked lowly.

"You think I'd bring a badge down here, Jack?" Fitch snorted. "He's an author."

"What's an author need to know about Nigel for?" Jigger inquired.

"He was pals with Nigel," Fitch said.

"Nigel wasn't pals with this pen worm," Jack scoffed.

"You're wrong, trumpet man," I said. "I knew him well enough to know what the law said he did is something he never would have done. Was he acting differently the last few times?"

None of them thought so.

"Where'd he work?" I asked.

"Brody's Diner," Character answered. "A dump on Central between Broadway and the railroad."

"He hang out anywhere in particular?"

"Not just anywhere," Jigger sneered. "He got in with the upper crust at this posh nightclub called The Parthenon."

"He ever say anything about a girlfriend?"

“Occasionally,” Fitch said. “A doll at that nightclub.”

“How long had he been seeing her?”

“End of last year was the first time he mentioned the doll,” Jigger said. “But he never gave her name or said what she looked like.”

This must have been the girl Nigel mentioned at the bakery last year and who had come by the boarding house. Why was he so loathe to tell anyone about her?

“He ever mention Bigelow?”

“Bigelow?” snorted Character. “Who’s Bigelow?”

“No Bigelow here,” Jack seconded.

“We need a pianist,” Jigger told me. “Sure you won’t try it?”

“Yeah, pen worm," said Character. "Put yourself to use. We're running mournful tunes, on account of Nigel."

"That racket when I came in wasn't mournful."

"That? Just a warm up," Jigger said. "What do you say? Start pounding the piano?"

"No dice."

“If it suits you, pal,” he shrugged. “Let’s give ‘When the Saints Go Marching In’ another push, George Lewis style, huh, fellas?”

The racket started up again. There was more to appreciate about this melody, but I got out before it could get me.

Brody's Diner was a rectangular slab of stucco with the name spelled out in turquoise letters at the top. The only lighting inside, save for the dismal daylight that oozed through dusty venetian blinds, came from filthy, flimsy circular lights dangling perilously from the stained ceiling.

Booths were by the windows, and a long counter was before a wall with black and white pictures of guys in swanky suits trying to look tough. Between the pictures was an opening into the kitchen, where a corpulent cook was dabbing his greasy face with a greasy towel and then using the towel to dry off some sickly vegetables he had pulled out of a pot of murky water. Above this opening was a long menu encompassed by grease and encased in plastic, with every item's price crossed off and rewritten in marker each time it increased.

A guy in a cheap suit was looking down at his phone in the middle booth, so I picked a stool near the doors. The rickety counter had everything you would expect a place like this to have – slimy menus, soiled napkins, condiments that weren't closed properly, crumbs along the corners, gum underneath, and that sickening smell of bleach and dirty tap water that some people actually thought cleaned anything.

At the other end of the counter, a high-schooler wearing a gold chain necklace was chatting up a chick with fake eyelashes and five pounds of makeup. A few minutes of waiting made me tired of looking at the slime and the dust and the decay.

“How about some service, Casanova?” I called.

He acknowledged my presence with an insouciant glance, straightened an untucked uniform shirt that draped over his diminutive frame, and arrogantly ambled over.

“What can I get you, *pal*?” the smurf said the last word like he had tasted something that was too disgusting even for this dump.

“One grilled cheese.”

“That’s the cheapest item on the menu, pal. What’s the matter? Running short on dough?”

"Where's Brody."

"Not very intuitive, are you, pal? You come into a place named Brody's, you see a greasy guy in the kitchen, and you see me. You think I'd own this dump?"

"It's too nice for you."

"That's rich, pal. Let's play a game of deduction. If I'm not Brody, and you're not Brody, and the guy in the booth isn't Brody, then that means the slimy stiff with the spatula *is* Brody. There he is in the flesh. He's got a lot of flesh, don't he?”

"I want to ask him something."

"You can ask me, pal. I'm a sharp character."

"I'll ask Brody."

"Maybe I don't feel like telling Brody, pal. What do you say to that?"

"Get me Brody, midget."

The smurf smirked and leaned his back against a counter in the opening on which Brody had set a plate of something that didn't look edible.

"Hey Brody," he sneered over his shoulder. "A jerk wants to talk to you."

"What jerk?" Brody snarled, now holding a cigarette between his yellow teeth.

"*This* jerk," the smurf stuck his tongue out at me.

"What do you want?" Brody growled.

"A little information," I replied, "about a guy who used to work here."

"For instance, who?" Brody spat and turned his broad, greasy back on me.

"For instance, Nigel Wilfred."

The moment the name came off my lips, Brody's gelatinous frame stiffened. He shifted uneasily, then turned around.

"How, how do you expect me to remember that?" he murmured once he had regained his boorish composure. "He was just some runt that worked here for a time. I didn't get chatty with him."

"When's the last time you saw him?"

"Why's it so important to you?" the fat guy sneered. "Were you his boyfriend?"

"He was my friend. Get to talking, or I'll beat you with one of those moldy carrots."

"That wouldn't be wise, Welles," a voice with a simultaneously suave and slimy cadence opined from behind me. I turned around to glance at the guy in the cheap suit I had seen looking down at his phone. Now, he was looking up at me.

"I said that wouldn't be wise, Welles," the guy grinned like the Chesire cat. "Didn't you hear me? You should speak when you're spoken to, Welles."

"Got my name, huh?"

He rose from the booth and took the stool next to mine. "I got a lot of things."

"Got a reason for not minding your own business?"

The guy chuckled with his front teeth plunged into his bottom lip, like a beaver. He was about thirty-five, with a sturdy build, a broad face, sneering silver eyes, blonde hair slicked back over his head, and a smirk that looked like he wore it often. His chin was dimpled and his smile was toothy and wide, like a sneering clown.

“You sound like you expect me to know something about this, Welles,” the guy lit a cigarette with his thumb and flicked the match off Brody’s back. “Kind of presumptuous of you, isn’t it?”

“What do you want?”

“What do I want?” he grinned even wider than before, following a puff. “What makes you think I want anything, Welles?”

I glanced back at Brody, who was alternating between picking his nose and sprinkling herbs onto a plate.

“I’m disappointed, Welles. They all say you’ve got good manners, but I’m not so sure I agree. It isn’t very nice to be abrupt with a guy doing you a favor.”

“A favor, huh?”

“Sure, Welles.”

The guy reached into his pocket and handed me a crisp, white card which read, *Matt Duryea, Private Investigations*, with an office address near the fair grounds, e-mail, and phone number.

When I returned the card, he gently placed it in a firm plastic seal and delicately put it back in his pocket, like he had just finished exhibiting a rare manuscript from an ancient culture.

"Wilfred happens to have stolen the thing I was hired to find – a jade statuette."

"Sure somebody else didn't steal it and put the finger on him?"

"Very sure."

"Who hired you?"

"I live by a code of honor, Welles. I uphold my clients' right to privacy. Now, if you gave me, say, ten grand, I'd think about letting names slip, but without any dough, I adhere to very rigid principles."

"A noble guy," I snorted.

"Now, Welles. I'm beginning to think you don't like me. Let's be reasonable. We're both asking about the same guy. You make my wallet a little bigger, and I'll drop some hints about Wilfred. How's it sound?"

I stared at Duryea while he curled one end of his lips like a pretzel and sneered out of the other end. A jade. What would

Nigel want with a jade? Why was he working in dumps like this, hanging around smugglers like Bigelow?

I swung around the slimy counter, marched past the smirking smurf, and pushed open the filthy swing doors that led to the kitchen.

“Get out of here,” Brody growled, wielding a flimsy spatula and beads of oily sweat.

I stuffed my hand into my coat pocket and made it look like I was aiming a gun at his gut.

“Wilfred, he, uh, he, came by that night."

"What night?"

"The night he combusted. I, I was in here, and, and, I mean, his shift was already done, and...”

“You expect me to believe that, fatso? Nigel worked the night shift.”

The fat guy grunted and gasped simultaneously. All four of his chins began to quiver.

“No, no, he didn’t,” Brody shook his head vehemently, sending ripples down the chunks of fleshly lard. “I’ll talk, I swear. Wilfred only worked here early afternoons. He always got off before five. The night, the night he croaked, he came by here around nine. Said he was in a jam. Said he needed dough.”

"What jam?"

"I, I don't know. Some guys were after him. Rough guys. Real rough guys. He wanted to blow and needed some cash. He was worried. These kind of characters, he wasn't used to dealing with them."

"What'd they want him for?"

"He wouldn't say. He wouldn't say nothing else about it."

"Who was with him?"

"No–nobody. But I didn't see everything. I just assume he came here on foot."

"This on the level?"

"Honest," Brody bleated.

I reached into my other pocket, took out a ten dollar bill, and tucked it into his greasy shirt.

"Your busboy know Nigel?"

"Yeah," Brody nodded toward a small door at the end of the kitchen. Behind it was a small office where the midget was kicked back in Brody's chair, pumping trap music through his speaker and vaping.

"Oh, that's right," the smurf sneered. "You were the jerk that wanted your service. Something about a sandwich, wasn't it?"

“How well did you know Nigel Wilfred?”

“Nigel Wilfred? I don’t know who that is. In case you're having trouble figuring it out, I'm on break, pal. This song is called 'Drip Too Hard', and I want to listen to it without having to look at you. Get out, pal.”

I recreated the fake gun to help jog his memory. When that didn’t take, I jerked him off the ground. The smurf’s smug demeanor quickly dissipated.

“I was never close with Wilfred,” he squealed. “We never hung out. I only saw him a few times because his shift ended when mine begins. The, the guy wasn’t my kind of company. I don't know what places he went. I never even knew where he lived. When he came by here that night he got it, I saw him on the way out. He said guys were after him. He was getting out of town.”

“Where was he going?”

“How would I know, pal? He wouldn’t tell me.”

“Who was with him?”

“Nobody.”

There wasn’t much sense waiting for whatever code-violating grub Brody would whip up, so I tipped the smurf similarly and headed into the dreary night.

8

THIEVES' HIGHWAY

The Parthenon made me feel like I had taken a time machine back to classical antiquity. Marble colonnades upheld a wide portico replete with ornate triglyphs; this was topped by a ravishing pediment populated by marble cartouches of Jove and Athena and Odysseus and Telemachus. Evenly spaced among the sturdy white bricks that constituted the building's body were Palladian windows, and between the cornices were marble figures of the muses.

A slender doorman in a tuxedo was standing in front of two wooden doors that must have weighed a hundred pounds each. Tar-colored hair slicked over the back of his head and curled at the nape.

“Name, please,” he said.

"Sinbad the Sailor."

"Nice try," the doorman smirked. "I was referring to your real name."

"Preston Welles."

"Welles, huh?" the doorman scrolled through an iPad. "Doesn't look like you're in our system. How'd you hear about us?"

"An enemy of a friend of an enemy."

"Might any of those characters be frequent patrons here?"

"Ask Bigelow. He ought to know."

The doorman scowled and tapped something on the iPad that made the doors open wide enough you could fit a yacht through.

"Don't try causing any trouble," he sneered. "Bigelow treats your type like a swatter treats flies."

The checkerboard tiles were as wide as trampolines. Metopes of Greek mythological characters were flanked on both walls by neoclassical landscape paintings and portraits of eighteenth century aristocrats. Candles stood atop iron poles and chandeliers dangled from an arched ceiling covered with Baroque frescoes. If Westminster Abbey was combined with the Sistine Chapel and shrunk down to a two-story building, it would look like this place.

I went through another pair of large doors and into a wide room with more candles and gilt chandeliers and the general atmosphere of an eighteenth century ballroom. There were more columns, more ornamented figurines on the walls and ceiling, more paintings and portraits, and a large fountain in the center, fashioned in the neoclassical style.

The bar, which reminded me of an eighteenth century tavern, stood against the east wall. I took the last stool on the left.

“You like drink?" asked the bartender, a thin Italian in a white longsleeve and a black vest.

“If I were thirsty.”

"Whas a matter, then? You gotta problem with-a the lady, eh? Thas not-a good. You keep the lady a-busy, so no time for-a fighting, eh? My wife, she give me plenty kids. She no gotta time for-a scolding me then. You try drink, eh?"

“Give me what Nigel Wilfred used to have, eh.”

The barkeep became as pale as St. Peter's Basilica.

“Ah, who?" he quickly sloshed a soaking rag across the counter. "Some-a-times, my hearing not so good, eh?"

“An old patron. In his early twenties, handsome, wavy brown hair, usually carried a gold pocket watch. Used to come here all the time, I hear.”

The bartender nervously glanced at a column in the corner. A meathead in a tuxedo stood there – a meathead in a tuxedo who had been watching my every movement.

"Ah, signor, you hear the one about-a the Irish gambler and-a the Scotch-a lawyer?"

“No.”

“You like hear the one about-a the Irish gambler and-a the Scotch-a lawyer?”

“No.”

“Ah. You hear the one about-a the blonde and-a the circus duck?”

“No.”

“You like hear the one about-a the blonde and the circus duck?”

“No.”

“Ah.”

"Quit acting like you didn't know Nigel," I said as I turned to my left. "When did you see him last?"

The Italian barkeep darted another furtive glance at the meathead in the tuxedo, then bent behind the counter.

"I see him the night he-a flame up," his voice sounded like it was coming from the bottom of a deep well. "He say he-a need to see Signor Bigelow. He-a very serious, Signor Wilfred. The whole time he-a sit here, he-a not be like-a himself. No-a smile. No-a laugh."

"How was he mixed up with Bigelow?"

"Signor Wilfred, he-a want his art displayed, eh. He-a know Signor Bigelow have-a Athena Society and lotta influence-a, eh. He-a know if-a Signor Bigelow display his art, he-a become famous, eh. Every-a day, he-a come in here begging Signor Bigelow about it, eh.

'Signor Bigelow,' say Signor Wilfred, 'just-a put up one-a my painting, eh. People will-a love it, eh.'

Signor Bigelow shake-a his head. 'Nothing-a doing. I gotta enough-a painting and it draw-a plenty.'

'But I-a do anything you say,' plead Signor Wilfred. 'I even help-a you with job-a if you need it. Just-a give-a my work a chance.'

'I-a think it over,' say Signor Bigelow."

"Think Bigelow killed him?" I asked casually.

"Ah, signor," the Italian had his back turned to me now. "I-a work for-a Signor Bigelow. He-a treat me well, eh. Signor Wilfred have-a issues, eh."

"What issues?" I asked sharply.

"Eh, he-a see a doctor. Name-a Chandler Murdoch. Signor Wilfred see him a long-a time."

Chandler Murdoch? That was the same guy Tyler G. Amthor wanted me to see.

“Was Nigel sick?” I frowned.

"Signor Wilfred have a difficulty find-a direction for his-a life. Signor Murdoch advise-a him."

"How long was Nigel going there?"

"Ah, many week. A two month, eh."

The meathead in the tuxedo ambled over to the counter and crunched my shoulder with a hand as big as a bear’s paw.

“New around here, aren’t you, twerp?” he sneered.

“Let go of my shoulder.”

“New around here, but you’re asking about dead guys that didn’t have anything to do with you.”

“Nigel was my friend. He had everything to do with me.”

The guy wrapped his meaty mitt around my forearm and yanked me off the stool like I was a rag doll.

“You know, Mr. Bigelow enjoys meeting new customers, twerp. Especially ones snooping into things that aren’t their business. What do you say we pay him a visit?”

"Appreciate the affection, lovely," I said as I pried his paw off, "but I'll let you know if I want to hold hands."

"Mr. Bigelow enjoys meeting new customers. Don't let's disappoint him."

I dragged my heels up a flight of elegant stairs and into an office with west-facing, eighteenth century bay windows which yielded a view of the city lights. Bookshelves along the south and north walls were filled with colorful books bound many moons before, and they were joined by two paintings: David's *The Death of Socrates* hung opposite Lorrain's *Seaport with the Embarkation of the Queen of Sheba*.

In the center of the room stood a glass desk, topped with a lamp and a laptop and a chariot clock and a bust of Cicero. A man was sitting behind that glass desk, holding a book bound with Moroccan binding and watching me with soft, silver eyes that looked like pawn shop beads after they'd been brought to a boil. He had a thin, blonde beard and thinner blonde hair that looked like wild grasses from a savannah. His olive-tinted skin clung tightly to his frame, and he wore a tailored, powder blue suit with a pink carnation in the right front pocket. This was Mr. Bigelow.

"Do you read Horace, Mr. Welles?" His voice was like the sound of biting into a fresh apple.

"Sure."

"Great minds of former years differed in their opinions of him. Dryden considered him a well-mannered court slave; Quintilian viewed his verse favorably. I prefer Ovid, but the *Odes* are sublime works of art, would you agree?"

"Jewels five words long, that on the stretched forefinger of all time sparkle forever."

"Very impressive to cite Tennyson as an authority," Bigelow smiled. "The philistines which populate this imbecilic modern age of ours truly have no excuse for their barbarous tastes, when cultured men like you and myself walk the world."

"The comparisons between us end there."

"Oh?" Bigelow raised his grassy eyebrows. "I suppose you mean that as an insult. I suggest sitting down while you criticize me. It's much more comfortable."

I sat down in a plush arm chair before the desk.

"I take it this is your first time in the Parthenon. A beautiful design, has it not?"

"You have good taste, for a smuggler."

Bigelow nodded blithely at Neville, who promptly slammed the back of my head with his knuckles.

"He's been asking about Nigel Wilfred," Neville told Bigelow as I tried to imagine the sensation wasn't as painful as it seemed. "Claimed they were pals."

"Interesting," Bigelow smiled again. "So, you were friends, were you? Surely, there must be something else motivating you besides that. You wouldn't happen to be a detective, would you, Mr. Welles?"

"If I were a detective, I'd know enough not to come here. They're all in your pocket, aren't they, Bigelow?"

The silver eyes became hard as concrete. Bigelow extracted a cigar from a gold case on the glass desk and lit a match.

"I suppose the police and I are on good terms," he replied cooly, after a puff. "But I don't know what you think soliciting for information about Wilfred here will accomplish."

"It'll help me find out who killed him, and why. You're the betting favorite."

"Don't you follow the news, Mr. Welles? Wilfred was a troubled young man, much like you seem to be. His vanity and hubris were responsible for his death, not myself or anything relating to me. Besides, if he were truly a friend of yours, as you claim, you should be well enough acquainted with his habits to know there..."

"Did he have the jade on him when you bumped him off? Or are you still looking for it?"

Shock flooded over Bigelow's face, so he puffed at his cigar until the normal expression returned.

"You apparently prefer hinting at things rather than saying them outright, Mr. Welles. You should give me a sufficient reason for your interest in Wilfred; otherwise, I might not think it judicious to allow you to continue disrupting my place of business."

"That what you call this racket?"

"I don't like your manners."

"I'm not crazy about yours."

"Don't make me correct you again, twerp," Neville sneered. His menacing bulk had been lurking at my back the whole time.

"This is a respectable establishment, Mr. Welles," Bigelow resumed. "I'd hate to..."

"You'd hate to give me what you gave Nigel."

"Since you seem to think I had something to do with Wilfred's death, then, yes. I'd hate to see you necessitate great harm upon yourself by conducting an unwarranted investigation of a closed case. It would be advisable for you to let the matter lie. Neville, see Mr. Welles to a private table. Ensure he has a very enjoyable evening, so long as he cooperates. My regards, Mr. Welles."

Neville showed me to a vacant table near a white grand piano toward the west wall, where a girl with her back turned was playing Chopin's *Aeolian Harp*. Something about her hair– a rich ebony tumbling down her head and back like curtains of ink – was familiar.

I knew now. She was Laura, the niece of Dudley Ridgley.

So, she had been Nigel's girlfriend. I could understand his telling me there was something different about her. I was seeing it for myself right now. And if Nigel would have gone to the ends of the earth with a girl, as he had vowed, this would be the one. This would be the Aphrodite in human flesh that inspired him to his greatest works.

"They should charge admission for these seats," I said when she was finished.

"Why?" Her voice was breathy and soft.

"They give you something you can't find just anywhere."

"What would that be?"

"You."

"Do you really think so?"

“I do.”

“What else do you think?” she asked as she closed the lid over the keys.

“About you?”

“About anything.”

“That’s kind of a broad topic. Suppose we narrow it down a bit.”

“But don’t make it about me.”

“What’s wrong with making it about you?”

“I don’t want to talk about it.”

“How about this place, then?”

“I wish I didn’t have to come here. I may quit soon and just work at the theater.”

“Not a bad idea. You put on a fine show.”

She looked astonished. "You've seen me perform?"

"Sure. I was there for on George M. Cohan night. Your plump uncle tried to introduce me to you after the play, but you didn't answer your door."

"I'm sorry. I wasn't myself that night. I didn't want to see anyone, since..."

"Since?"

"Since he," was all she could get out before she turned away.

“Nigel?”

“Yes,” her eyes widened with surprise. “How did you know?”

“A hunch. He happened to be my friend.”

“You?”

“Preston Welles. I know, you never heard of me.”

I explained the rest to her. She didn’t seem to know any more about Nigel helping Bigelow get a jade than the Italian barkeep did.

“I suspect Whit,” Laura said. “The last thing Nigel told me was he would meet Whit here before coming to the theater. When he never showed up, I knew something had happened. Perhaps that’s why I was so afraid that night. My anxiety was so strong, I could hardly perform. I tried to call him when the play was done, but he didn’t answer. I locked myself in my room and cried. I heard my uncle knocking, but I was too upset to see him.”

She didn’t seem anxious when I saw her performing.

“The Italian at the bar said Nigel was seeing a psychiatrist named Chandler Murdoch. Ever heard of him?”

"No," Laura said slowly. "I didn't think Nigel would want to see a psychiatrist."

She lowered her head and looked away. I'd pumped her enough, for now.

I scrolled my phone number on a napkin and handed it to her, and she gave me her number. "We can get together at a better time. We seem to be the only two that cared for him."

"It was nice meeting you," she told me as she folded the napkin fretfully, like a child. "I wish Nigel had told you he had come back to Albuquerque sooner. Maybe things would be, would be..."

The welling of a tear appeared in her right eye, but she wiped it away and gently shook her head.

That was all I could do myself. I went home and thought about old times and wished things that weren't so were so, and that things that were so weren't so. Poor Nigel.

But what of that psychiatrist he was seeing? I took out the card Tyler G. Amthor had given me and looked at it. *Chandler Murdoch, Transpersonal Psychiatry*. Faint Oriental font. An office in his own house.

For the next ten minutes, I scrolled through his website. Each webpage had a background of multi-colored, three dimensional patterns that seemed hypnotic. An obnoxious humming sound like "ohum" droned on in the background, but that wasn't the only part that repulsed me. There was the pseudo-spiritual palaver and preposterous promises and spurious testimonies and occultic overtones. There was the recurring theme of employing "the sacred divinity of the soul" to solve all of mankind's woes.

Chandler Murdoch, Transpersonal Psychiatry. It didn't matter what your problems were. With the sacred divinity of the soul, and a regularly recurring bushel of your money, he could cure a leper and transform a juvenile delinquent into a Rhodes scholar and summon a rainstorm and raise the levels of the Rio Grande and stop a plague of locusts. All things were possible to him that believed in Murdoch, the Great and Powerful.

Chandler Murdoch, Transpersonal Psychiatry. The sacred divinity of the soul. The man that could work miracles. I decided to pay him a visit.

9

XANADU

Chandler Murdoch perpetuated the sacred divinity of the soul from a two-story house off Spruce Street and Roma Avenue. Behind an ornamented iron gate, a curving driveway was flanked by lush grass and red-leaf Photinias and Japanese primroses. Sour morning sunlight that looked like it that had been dropped through a strainer streamed through the majestic Black Pine and Nilgiri trees which stood back of the house. The grass ended at a brown brick walkway, which weaved past hydrangeas and spotted laurel shrubs and bonsai trees and vines to a small portico.

A deep daffodil house stared solemnly down at me. Its brick red, gable and hip roof was designed like the top of a pagoda and surmounted with a silver Chinese dragon in place of a weathercock. The shoji windows had vermilion trim and, with the exception of a window by the front door, were shut.

I pulled a gilt ring in a dragon's head mounted right of a traditional Chinese door, prompting the singular echoes of a

Chinese gong to reverberate throughout the house. A little Chinese man in his forties wearing a Zhongshan suit – the same suit I'd seen in Nigel's closet – answered the door with a simper.

"Excuse please. You are?"

"Murdoch around?"

"Mr. Murdoch busy man. You are?"

"A friend of Nigel Wilfred. Tell Murdoch I want to see him."

"You are detective, no?"

"I am detective, no. I am friend of Nigel Wilfred, yes. I like see Murdoch."

"Excuse please."

The little man shut the door. Stone lions and laughing Buddha statues were arranged on the porch in pairs; to their right was a flowerbed of asters and jasmine. Good luck gongs dangled from the front door, and Japanese bamboo stalks were growing to its left.

A few minutes later, the little man opened the door again.

"Mr. Murdoch very busy man," he started to close the door. "You come in different time."

I pushed the door open. "I come in this time."

A sickly aroma hung in the foyer's air and gave my stomach a whirl. I clenched my teeth just in time to keep it down.

"Haw haw," the little man snickered. "Those who come without invitation have difficult experience. Stranger should not force into Mr. Murdoch house. Stranger should learn not underestimate surrounding."

"Skip the philosophy lesson, Confucius," I snorted. "Where's Murdoch?"

"Stranger follow this way."

The little man opened the first door on the right, and I went father into the Far East.

There was a bronze Buddha head, some figurines of elephants, gilt encasements of swords and sabers and spears, rich tapestries of great kingdoms, Hindu temple carvings of snake charmers, paintings limning geishas at tea and great warriors in battle, sketches of pagodas in sultry fog, enormous rugs with curious patterns, statuettes of Hindu gods, scroll paintings of white peacocks, and a silk tapestry of Chinese damsels playing Wie Qi. Pots along a large, south-facing window with maroon curtains featured lotus, orchids, lilies, and pearl Indian hawthorn. A Chinese grandfather clock sounded with nine gongs.

Xanadu in a drawing room. A jade statuette that Bigelow wanted Nigel to steal seemed like it would fit right in with the rest of these things. I suspected it had.

The little man simpered again. "Mr. Murdoch very busy man."

"You said that already. I'm not leaving until I see him."

The little man snickered, sneered, and walked out of the room with short, straight steps. Walking out of here wasn't a bad idea, because this room, and the atmosphere that was heavier than lead, and the feeling of being watched by every statuette and bust and figurine and tapestry in it, gave me the creeps. Why would anybody sit in here? How could anybody sit in here?

I was walking out when a prominently displayed painting caught my eye. Although neoclassical in style, it depicted a scene in the Orient. A European in a tang suit was addressing several peasants in a rice field, with a Chinese-styled house, towering cypress trees, and a distant mountain peak in the background. The strips of sky not covered by storm clouds were tinted magenta.

"Very beautiful, is it not?" asked a voluptuous voice.

A patrician, half-Chinese brunette wearing a red cheongsam stood at the threshold above the living room, holding a few baby's breath in delicate hands.

"Do you like this style?" she asked me, those almond eyes locked on mine, her mellifluous voice more prominent than before.

I said I liked this style.

"The old masters were so much more precise with their craft. Their aim was to express themselves profoundly, to produce only the noblest art of which they were capable. This desire bears itself out in beauteous ways."

"Too bad one of them never painted you."

Her almond eyes flickered sultrily and front teeth as white as plaster sank into her glossy bottom lip. "You're waiting for my husband, aren't you?"

"How'd you guess?"

"Lots of people wait for my husband."

"Including you?"

"Especially me."

"Is the wait worth it?"

"It depends on what you're waiting for. If you're waiting for treatment, like his patients do, I'd say no. If you're waiting for romance, like I do, I'd say definitely no."

"I'm not waiting for either. Think that means I'll get what I'm looking for?"

"I doubt it."

She sauntered into the living room and exhibited her comely curvature on a wooden Chinese chair that looked as comfortable as concrete. At her prompting, I opted for a padded bench opposite it.

"We might as well introduce ourselves," she said as she selected a cigarette from a gilded case and flicked a gold lighter. "My name is Amelia."

"I'm Preston Welles."

"Preston Welles? A handsome guy with a handsome name."

"Much obliged."

Amelia blew smoke sensually and leaned back. She plucked a camellia out of its pot and began rubbing her fingertips across it. Then she adjusted her hair, which was pinned up like brown silk. Then she showed me that fine face in all its sublimity and smiled.

"What does Preston Welles need to see my husband for, if he isn't a patient? I can't think of any reason anyone would want to see my husband, especially if he isn't a patient."

"I want to talk to him about Nigel Wilfred."

"Who? Oh, yes, the nice young man."

"See much of him?"

"A couple of times. He always had something pleasant to say to me."

"Seem like there was anything wrong with him?"

"Not to me," she puffed. "But you don't know my husband. Everybody always has something wrong with them, and *he's* the only one that can fix it."

"Who gave him the Zhongshan suit?"

Amelia smiled with satisfaction. "I did."

"Did he steal a jade from here?"

"Him, steal? Certainly not. My husband affects tolerance, but he would never counsel somebody he suspected of theft."

"Crazy about your husband, aren't you?"

"I adore him."

"You must have riveting conversation."

"Riveting enough to cure insomnia. And once he gets going on his psychobabble? Forget it."

"All I need from him is whatever he knows about Nigel."

"Don't get your hopes high," Amelia snorted. "He won't tell you anything about Nigel that you haven't heard already."

"I don't believe what I've heard already. That's why I'm up here."

"So, you're conducting your own investigation?"

"It's the least I can do."

A well-built, part-Mongolian man in his mid-thirties wearing a yukata and a sadistic smirk appeared at the threshold and surveyed me with beady brown eyes that looked like they enjoyed seeing pain inflicted.

"Mr. Murdoch will see you now, friend," he announced. His voice was like sandpaper that had been left out in the rain.

I ignored him and turned back to the brunette. "When's the last time you saw Nigel?"

"A week ago."

"Was he acting any differently then?"

"He was the same as usual. I went to get some fresh air – that's what I call getting out of this fly trap – for a couple of hours, and when I came back, he was walking to his car. We spoke briefly, and he left."

"His car?" I frowned.

"Yes, it was a Porsche, I believe. A very nice model. He always kept it in good condition."

"You're sure it was his car?"

"Certainly. He always referred to it as such; why should I doubt him? Nigel was a very truthful person."

I leaned back against the bench. Something wasn't adding up. Nigel coming to a nutty joint like this, driving a Porsche, while living at a boarding house and getting meager dough from a dumpy diner. Somebody was selling me a lot of bunk. Maybe they all were.

The burly messenger kept standing at threshold, the atmosphere kept weighing me down like a lead curtain, the eerie antiques kept watching me, and Amelia kept swirling smoke around.

"Mr. Murdoch does not like waiting, friend," the half-Mongolian announced curtly.

"I'll be seeing you, then," I told her as I rose and took the fleshy hand she extended toward me. "I have a hunch I'll like your husband's company a lot less than I like yours."

"I'd say the same, from personal experience. Come see me again, won't you?"

"Your husband might not like that."

"But I might."

I left her smiling seductively up at me and went to the threshold, where the burly messenger was standing in the same stiff posture as he had been the whole time. He must have had a strong core.

"I'll be seeing Murdoch now, friend," I smirked.

The guy turned on his heels like a statue and lumbered down a long, strange hall filled with fixtures that threw distorted light through murky prisms and paintings of Japanese emperors and wallpaper of lotuses and wax figures wearing Korean armor and wielding redoubtable blades.

"Mr. Murdoch does not appreciate your actions, friend," the burly messenger remarked. "The impropriety of your coming here uninvited is intensified by your making him wait."

"I made him wait, huh?"

"Each second he deviates from communing with the great spirit of illumination hinders the development of his divinity. It is very noxious to his enlightenment and meditative conscience, friend."

"You sound like you expect me to know what that means."

"Every soul understands these things, friend. They are as native to a man's breast as the act of breathing."

"Think so?"

"Yes, friend. I suggest you refrain from exhibiting your manifest contempt of these topics while in the presence of Mr. Murdoch."

At the end of the hall, on the right side, was a thick door with Thai patterns that almost looked three-dimensional. The burly messenger opened this to a room with a high ceiling and two enormous, east-facing windows that threw a strange tint on the sunlight that poured through them. The atmosphere in here was twice as heavy as the one out there; the sickly aroma was even worse.

Between the windows was a wooden desk that weighed more than a slab from Stonehenge. On this stood a bizarre lamp that looked like a stalk, and gilt cases, and a marble dragon, and an iPad in a case that had probably been made from a Bengal tiger's hide. Gongs dangled on the wall directly behind the desk, and in the northeast corner, a wax figure wearing a kamishimo stood strangely in the sunlight.

More maroon curtains slithered at the sides of the windows, and between them stood two tall bookshelves stocked with old books and old manuscripts and occasionally a jar of fish whose eyes bulged out of their sockets, or a glass of unsightly bugs that looked like they were jockeying for position in case somebody lifted the lid.

But the strangest thing in the room was the man in the scarlet shenyi who had been watching my every movement since I entered. He sat behind the desk in a scarlet chair shaped like a Thai throne, observing me with yellow eyes that felt like they were penetrating my soul. He could have been twenty or sixty, because something singularly strange in his face made him look young and old at the same time.

Maybe it was the chrome hair which had been shaved everywhere except for an inch-wide, braided bundle that tapered down the center of his head into a Chinese pigtail. Maybe it was the lips that looked luminous in the sun. Maybe it was the bizarre hue that clung to his skin, as if it were phosphorescent. Maybe it was that his whole head was shaped and glowed like an iridescent lightbulb.

Nothing I could say or do would surprise him. I could leap onto the table, take two barracudas out of my pockets, swallow them whole, and sing "I'm Just Wild About Harry", and he wouldn't flinch. He was as unflappable as the stone lions on his porch. Maybe that was why Tyler G. Amthor thought he was such a sage.

"You must be Preston Welles," Murdoch said, with a voice that was faint and loud at the same time and smacked of disgustingly artificial tranquility. He took a strangely shaped hand out from under the desk and weaved an odd gesture with it, like he was conducting an invisible orchestra.

I said I was Preston Welles.

Murdoch spent thirty seconds emitting a slow, musical breath. Then he rubbed his fingertips across his eyebrows and made prolonged "ohum" sounds like those from his website. Then he held his arms out perpendicularly and opened his mouth and dragged a large tongue in a counterclockwise orbit. Then he fixed his yellow eyes back on my soul.

"I should have preferred you placed an appointment before entering. The unsolicited presence of judgemental bigotry always interferes with my mindfulness and disturbs my meditative wavelengths."

"It also spoils the milk and ruins the crops and dries out the river and makes the mice squeak."

"Mockery is most undesirable. Howbeit, I am pleased to make your acquaintance, my good soul. Use that chair to relieve your standing."

He repeated the gesture, this time directing it at another one of those Chinese chairs Amelia had been sitting in. Then, he took out the other hand and folded it against the first one.

"Relieve is a funny word for it," I said as I tried to find a part of the chair that didn't feel like leaning against cinderblock.

"Strange, what things elicit humor from our hearts. The Hatatarogo have a practice of *yayunshibud*, whereby a visitor who arrives without notice or invitation is clubbed, stretched on a rack, dipped into boiling water, tied with vines, and left to be devoured by wild beasts."

"Sounds serious."

"All things are serious to the enlightened mind, be it a recompense for impropriety, or a code of honor which Western man would do well to use. Yet, it is no wonder that enlightenment escapes him, when toxic, confusing energy perpetually plunders his soul's sacred stimuli. Purge the impurity that suppresses the soul, and only cosmic depth and theosophical tranquility remain to buttress our inner beings."

"Just like that, huh?" I snorted.

"Naturally. Within all of us lies the divinity of spirit by which we may ascend to loftier plains of consciousness. Within all of us, the pureness of heart and mind by which we may become one with the spirits and the gods. Yet, it is by our commitment to tolerance, and not judgement; acceptance, and not discernment; and tranquility, and not dogmatism, that we chart the course which shall constitute our sacred journey through this solemn sphere. Consider the young plant in the forest. Occluded from the light by fellow vegetation, it remains undergrown and stagnant. But remove the fetters prohibiting its growth, and rapid enlightenment stimulates its tendrils. Understanding and mindfulness personify its stems. And from thence it rises above the base acts of self-determination and intolerant bigotry to bask in the glow of enlightenment."

I glanced at the gilt clock on the wall and yawned. Murdoch held up one of his hands like he was directing traffic.

"Forebear at feigning interest. Only a few elect souls truly share delight in such subjects. Only a few elect souls perceive the human soul is a delicate object which requires both strength and grace to understand, to be cultivated and conveyed in ways pleasing and divine. But men of the East readily comprehend this concept. I spent years among them gleaning the follies by which Western man clumsily attempts to bludgeon wisdom out of something that must be handled gently, with delicacy, with..."

"How long had Nigel Wilfred been coming here?"

Murdoch smiled by folding his upper lip upward and bottom lip downward to reveal teeth I could practically see my reflection in. It was a sickly smile. It was a smile that could watch a man get ripped apart by lions and not lose its form, a smile that could witness every form of sadism and bloodshed conceivable and remain undisturbed.

He hovered a hand over a dish covered by an embroidered lid. Under the lid was a live, blue beetle as long as a compass, which he methodically ground to powder over a saucer. Then, he raised the saucer, tipped its contents into his mouth, and looked at me with unsettling satisfaction.

"Yang tells me you spoke of deep friendship with Nigel. Deep friendship always engenders familiarity with the other's habits and desires. You should know how long he had been coming here."

"If I did, I wouldn't be talking to you."

"Your judgmental air is noxious to me," Murdoch mewled. "But I will tolerate it, for Nigel was a favorite patient of mine, and I shall view favorably those who claim to be his friends. Such a shame that he could not conquer the passions that drove him to ruin, that he could not bridle the desires that granted his destruction. When Nigel first came to me, about six months ago, I saw his soul was unstable by reason of his desires. He had not conquered the will to brutality which so personifies Western man. Moreover, he was unsettled on what course he was to pursue within this weary world of bigotry and intolerance. I attempted to shape his thoughts by imparting Eastern wisdom and vibrative patterns."

"That all you did?"

"Would you care to explain what you imply by that remark?"

"You seem to have the answers to everything. Why don't you figure it out?"

Murdoch sighed with the sonorous pitch of a ringing gong. "I see one similarity already between Nigel and yourself, and that is your shared unsoundness of mind and constitution. When was the most recent occasion you received psychiatric care, Mr. Welles?"

"Never."

"I see. There is no need to feel ashamed over your condition. Many sincere souls are troubled with the burdens of disorder through no fault of their own. Oftentimes, they do not even realize how troubled they are, and become belligerent in denying reality. Strongly consider enlisting my services while your disorders are but mild. What you struggle with can be remedied, but it requires much time for the transformation to effectuate. Without knowledge of the sacred divinity of the soul, a man is inhibited from reaching the sublime enlightenment of soul consciousness which is the ultimate purpose for existence. Why not begin our first session now, while you remain enchanted by the wholesome forces around you? I offer you a free analysis today, but forthcoming appointments shall require $950 each."

"Why not charge a grand even?"

"Sneering sarcasm personifies an unbalanced soul. Could your judgmental impressions be compelling you to reject the very thing your soul most earnestly seeks?"

"Did Nigel steal your jade?"

"What brought that idea to you, my good soul?"

"Did Nigel steal your jade?"

Murdoch rose from his throne and took long, silent strides into full view. He couldn't have been more than 6' 2", but he looked like his head would go through the ceiling if he stood on his tiptoes. His bare feet were oblong and uneven, like mountains, and he walked on them like he expected the ground to give out underneath him at any minute.

"I owe to all my patients, both living and dead, the pious privacy to which every soul's private conversation is entitled. What passed between Nigel and myself, except for what may profit your soul's enlightenment, must remain between us. Besides, one can never tell what baleful things will redound from sharing such information with an unenlightened manufacturer of close-minded bigotry as yourself."

Murdoch retrieved the jar of fish and crossed a Persian rug as big as a helipad and held the jar a foot from me. Their eyes were bulging more prominently than they had appeared from afar. I was getting more uneasy by the minute.

"These fish were once in a similar situation to yourself, Mr. Welles," Murdoch said as I got up from the chair. "They drifted through the sea of their days without regard for the development of their inner consciousness. Doubtless, they supposed no harm would befall them in their native state. But the grasping hand of man seized them without warning and packed them into this jar without mercy. And now, they stare into an eternity of blank regret, without any means of correcting their course. If you do not rectify the recondite errors which plague your soul, I foresee your enduring an equally pernicious fate."

"I don't think I'd fit in that jar."

"Your every word condemns the insanity implicit within your heart," Murdoch scoffed. "It proves what I have been speaking of to be true – that you are unsound and dangerous. The longer your reject the nourishment so necessary to your soul, the longer you shunt it from the sacred paths of peace which it yearns to experience. I request that you do not call again, unless you will submit yourself to the stimulating rapture of enlightenment I offer. If you seek to learn more about Nigel, I suggest you solicit a psychic, or some other spiritualist who can enable you to contact him more capably than I can. I wish you radiant contentment, Mr. Welles."

The burly messenger was waiting for me in the hall, standing with that same stiff posture, leering at me with those same serpentine eyes.

"Think I'm unsound and dangerous?" I snickered.

"You are whatever Mr. Murdoch pronounces you to be, friend. If that is what he has determined you are, then that is what you are."

"If he determined I were a walrus with five heads and feet like a koala, that's what I would be, huh?"

"Precisely, friend."

I went back down the long, strange hall with the fixtures that threw funny light around and the weird wallpaper and the paintings of emperors and the wax figures that looked like they would slice me to matchsticks if I pulled a fast one. Amelia wasn't in the living room, so I let myself out and enjoyed the first light air I'd inhaled since I went inside.

Nigel had lived in a boarding house, worked at a diner, sought a jade for a goods smuggler, yet he drove a Porsche and pocketed enough dough to pay this worm for frequent visits. The only scenario that seemed possible was Bigelow sending him there and paying for the appointments so Nigel could scout the place and swipe the jade easily. But nobody there had given a hint that Nigel had stolen anything.

I spun my mind while my car spun its wheels, then turned around and headed for Matt Duryea's office.

10

THE ASPHALT JUNGLE

Would Nigel really hang around a weirdo like Murdoch for six months just to have a chance at stealing his jade? I was wont to think so, when I remembered his vehement declaration in his grandfather's library that "my art is my purpose for existence." If he would give his very soul to ensure the immortality of his art, then he would have no qualms over stealing a jade to catapult his career.

I spent the entire drive down to Duryea's wondering why every psychiatrist I'd ever encountered was either a vain fop that wasn't half as smart as he thought he was, or a deranged, disturbed maniac that belonged in a dungeon. And to think millions of people look to those crackpots for wisdom and guidance in life.

While I mulled this over, I remembered that Nigel's noble nature was vulnerable to indulging dishonorable acts. There had been desperation in his brooding expression at the bakery, desperation to do whatever was necessary to see his art was displayed. I'd seen the look before.

Not long after I had met Edgar Graham, Nigel and I were at the annual Burqueno Art Festival, where his gorgeous painting of an opulent neighborhood south of Old Town was among the many exhibits vying for a thousand dollar prize and statewide recognition.

Nigel's lofty landscape easily excelled the drab and inane works which surrounded it, but I knew better, in this age of enlightened idiots, than to expect beauty and style to win out over tasteless trash and "heroic" expressions of barbarity. After all, the modern man is accustomed to call the hatred of beautiful things "progress", and designate the embrace of vile and vacuous garbage as "taste" and "appreciating true art." What a world.

"I like yours the best, Nigel, but I don't think it will win," I said as we stood observing the collection arranged on an orange wall.

"I don't think it will, either," he bitterly replied. "In fact, I know it won't. It's simply too profound to be appreciated by any of these insipid stooges that will evaluate it."

"A shame," I shook my head. "Sure, the dough is decent, but the prestige of winning something like this and getting a good shine on your name is invaluable. Especially while you're still at university."

Nigel nibbled at the side of his upper lip as he always did whenever nervous or doubtful about something important. Then, his eyes shone with the sparkle of a scheme. Nigel straightened his tie and wearily approached Ms. Emily Drum, a middle-aged woman with a buzzcut who was one of the judges. He stopped five feet away and faced me.

"Oh, what's the use!" he sobbed. "I gave it my best, but my painting will never win. I, I should like to withdraw it from the contest. I don't believe it deserves to be included."

Drum scowled through her glasses and looked Nigel over.

"I promised Father I would be better than this," Nigel said earnestly, after glancing in the reflection of a nearby display case to make sure he had captured Drum's attention. "You were there, Welles, when he asked, with his dying breath, that I make myself a great artist. I promised him I would. And what do I do with myself? I produce something which scarcely deserves to be compared with the sterling artistry that surrounds it. Take the painting to its right. Mine portrays a neighborhood with bland reality; this painting, however, is fascinating. I can't make any of it out, and that excites me. My work is boring and ordinary; the other one, brilliant and singular."

Nigel turned to Drum, pretending to mistake her for a museum patron.

"Don't your agree, ma'am? Don't you agree that my landscape painting pales in comparison to the great works of art beside it?"

Drum looked at them like someone well versed in staring blankly at a painting while pretending to analyze its every square inch. After a few minutes, she slowly glanced at myself, then at Nigel.

"I admire your honesty," she said affectedly, "and your perception. How old are you?"

"Twenty-one," Nigel replied.

"To be that discerning at twenty-one? Very admirable. Do you really want your painting removed?"

"Yes. It doesn't belong with the rest of them. I painted it because I thought Father would appreciate its style, but that was before, before..."

Nigel followed with another impassioned sob.

"Don't be discouraged, young man," Drum patted him on the shoulder like a woman that didn't know how to perform woman's most inherent instinct of gentleness. "Your painting doesn't compare with the others, but it isn't as bad as you say. What's your name?"

He told her his name, and she waddled to a small door in the orange wall. When she came out, something resembling a smile was spread across her ogre-like face.

"I've had a word with the other judge," Drum said. "We decided your earnestness in spite of the loss of your father matters more than the quality of your painting. You're the winner."

"I am?"

"Congratulations, Mr. Wilfred. In our original tally, your painting finished fourth because it lacked the creativity and ingenious style of the ones next to it. But both I and the other judge believe that one's motive and worldview matter more than the quality of art they produce, and that art should be judged by the character of its creator, rather than by the art itself. I happen to know the three artists who would have finished ahead of you have been rude to me on numerous occasions, even though we agree modern craft is far superior to those obsolete, oppressive older methods."

"Hooray for the winners," I said as Drum waddled away. "Where did you get that yarn?"

"I'd that little speech in mind only after we discussed how unlikely I was to win," Nigel replied as cooly as if the lie had been the truth. "When opportunity presented itself, I gladly took advantage. And now my name will shine on the roll of fame."

"But to lie, Nigel. And about your father, no less."

"Pragmatism is the surest means of success," he shrugged. "The means, though unpleasant, can justify the end, if noble. Now that I have won, you will see."

He was right, in a way. He appeared in every art publication in the Southwest and was invited to a gala in Los Angeles to celebrate the honor. An art critic there was so impressed with Nigel's painting that he recommended casting around the upper echelon of art displays in Albuquerque to see whether they would take his work.

At some point between then and our last meeting, Nigel had encountered Bigelow, decided he would do whatever was necessary to get him to display his paintings, and the rest was history. I'd forgotten this, and several other anecdotes like it, during my initial wave of grief. I'd forgotten that if Nigel wanted something desperately, he would do whatever he thought necessary to obtain it. But that still didn't explain why Murdoch made no mention of the jade.

Duryea was kicked back in a padded black chair, putting his shoes up on a desk that had very little on it besides a laptop, a lamp, and a stack of folders. With his right hand, he was holding a shot glass that was about a quarter full, and with his left hand, he was holding a whiskey bottle. His face was full of that toothy smirk I couldn't stand, even though I'd only seen it once before. Beside the desk, a small speaker played Beethoven's *Eighth Symphony*.

"Now, Welles," he took a swig of the rotten stuff and set his drinking instruments in a small cabinet to the left. "I knew they all say you're a gentleman, but I didn't think you'd condescend to paying little old me a visit."

There was another cabinet, open and full of liquor, mounted halfway up the opposite wall. Along the baseboard beneath it, Duryea's detective license was framed and collecting dust, like a forgotten relic in an old museum.

Two tall, narrow, east-facing windows provided scenic views of a parking lot covered in everything from weeds to hypodermic needles to human waste, and whatever crawled along the sidewalks of San Pedro Drive a few blocks north of Central.

"I wish my office wasn't the first door when you come in," Duryea snickered. "Then maybe you'd get to meet some of the nice freaks that keep shop here. Some of the gorgeous freaks. They smell real nice."

"Do they smell as nice as Chandler Murdoch?"

The sneer disappeared from Duryea's face as much as it could from a guy who was always sneering. His eyes became as hard as bricks.

"Who's that?"

"You wanted ten G's just to tell me his name. Don't tell me you've forgotten already."

"So you figured it out. What do you want for it? A pat on the back? A handshake? A big, toothy grin?"

“Murdoch wouldn’t have bothered hiring a rat like you if he already knew Nigel had the jade. What makes you so sure he did?”

“Sure?" Duryea sneered. "I never said I was sure, Welles. I just said he happened to steal the jade I was hired to find. My guess is he set himself up with Murdoch because he had the place scouted and wanted an easy in.”

“You're forgetting Bigelow paid for the appointments. Nigel only took the jade so Bigelow would display his paintings."

“Wilfred was still the guy that stole it. Sure, Bigelow sent him up there on false pretenses, but Wilfred still swiped the jade. Well, almost false pretenses.”

“What’s that supposed to mean?”

“Now, Welles. You’re disappointing me again. I thought writers had great powers of observation. They can sniff a gnat from a mile away. Don’t tell me you didn’t see the dame.”

“Amelia?”

“So, you even know her name. Maybe I spoke too soon, Welles. Maybe you aren’t so dull after all. Did you figure out your pal was seeing her by intuition, or did she have to sit in your lap first?”

I reached across the desk, grabbed a handful of Duryea’s collar, and walloped him against the wall. He snickered as he straightened his hair, then went back to the chair and put his shoes back on the desk. The sneer returned.

"Nigel didn't go for her type," I said.

"No?" Duryea lit a cigarette with his thumb and flicked the match off my shirt. "Why do you suppose he kept going up there, Welles? It doesn't take a character like Wilfred long to figure things out. He fingered the jade from the get go and kept riding those appointments so he could see her on the side. Then she got sore and told Murdoch and he had your pal bumped off. But I didn't look too much into that. I was only hired to find the jade, you know."

I walked over to one of the windows and looked out at the nasty parking lot and the ugly sidewalk and the dismal street and the sullen day and the sleazy parties going by. Nigel, a jade thief and a Casanova?

"I don't know what your romantic situation is, Welles," Duryea slithered, "but I hear Murdoch's dame is there for the taking, if you like the backstabbing type. You know, just between the two of us, I wonder if Wilfred wanted to run off with her. Maybe that's why he never got Bigelow the jade."

"How do you know Bigelow didn't get the jade?"

"He happened to send a couple of his gentlemen over here morning before last asking about it. Very respectable people,

Bigelow's guys. They didn't even threaten to kill me if I didn't tell them anything."

If Nigel really had taken the jade – something that seemed more likely by the minute – and hadn't given it to Bigelow, the latter must have frisked the boarding house. But what did Nigel do with it?

"Don't believe me, do you, Welles?" Duryea sneered. "Then go pay Schuler's Shop a visit yourself. It's not too far from here. You might even consider walking. Ought to introduce you to some very colorful personalities. You'd have a blast with those characters, Welles."

"You imply Murdoch bumped Nigel off out of jealousy, retrieved the jade, then hired you to cover his tracks."

"Really, Welles. I may be a boor, but I'm a respectable boor. Why would a quack like Murdoch go to the trouble of doing that when the law was never connecting him to it in the first place?"

I ran a hand through my hair and shook my head. My thoughts were making less sense by the minute. Duryea detected this and puffed proudly.

"Kind of hard to think straight, isn't it, Welles? Especially when you're trying to trick yourself into thinking stuff that wasn't so. Your pal wasn't so great, you know. Maybe he was when you two were in knee pads, but guys can change, Welles, especially when they're running around with smugglers. That takes an effect on the mind. Makes a guy think about doing things he wouldn't even consider. Now, he's not such a great guy anymore. Now, he's a hood and a mobster, just like his new friends. Now, he's a cheap..."

I couldn't help myself. I grabbed another handful of collar, walloped against him against the wall again, and watched with contempt as he snickered and straightened his hair and went back to the chair and put the shoes back on his desk and put the sneer back on his face.

"I don't like people taking me for a punching bag, Welles. If you keep doing it, I might think about pressing charges. You look worn out. Why don't you relax? Get yourself a nice lady and take the rest of the day off. What do you care about a bum jade, anyway? I don't think it should interest you. I don't think it should interest you even if Amelia Murdoch dropped it between her..."

I went forward to perform act three, but inexplicably stopped myself.

"That's better, Welles," Duryea's sneer widened as he took another puff. "We're making progress, aren't we? Why, by tomorrow, you might even be able to walk down the street without socking the first guy that suggests your pal wasn't an angel. I guess I was wrong. Miracles really do happen."

11

THE NAKED CITY

I felt like I had been going in circles. Why would Bigelow have killed Nigel if he didn't know where he was keeping the jade? Why would Murdoch have hired Duryea if he killed Nigel and retrieved the jade? If Nigel had taken the jade for Bigelow, why did he run off with it, and who did he give it to? All I knew for sure was I had tied my brain into a pretzel trying to figure everything out.

But out of the blue, I thought of an October afternoon two years ago, when Nigel had returned to visit his grandparents, and we were loitering about the scrub of the Sandia Heights landscape before their courtyard.

I had stopped by on my way back from a day at the Nichols – perhaps it was the same day that Abigail Nichols had tricked me into meeting M.K. Matthewson at his office, since the earth was damp from rain and the unappreciable autumn sun was casting everything in a cheerless light.

"I'm very happy to hear of your good fortune, Welles," Nigel smiled, referencing my job at the *Enchantment Times* and the forthcoming publication of my first book. "I always knew that genius burned within your breast. When will this novel of yours be available? I should love to read it."

"Bucy said by Christmas."

"How exhilarating it will feel to see a book in print with your name on it," he poked a stick at a rock. "And what of this Abigail Nichols? Fair damsel, I should say."

"She makes Aphrodite look like Hillary Clinton."

"What a profitable turn of events, Welles. In a matter of months, your literary career is established, your first novel leaps off the presses, your name shines lustrously on the roll of fame, and a beautiful woman awaits you while you work in a palace. A dream job! A dream life!"

"A dream job? Please don't call it that. That term reeks too much of modernity. Call it a fulfilled fantasy."

"Very well," Nigel nodded. "A fulfilled fantasy. Do you suppose your wedding approaches?"

"Not if her old man has anything to say about it," I snorted. "He sicced the law on me in the summer when a blackmailer named Bankins crashed into the Rio Grande. I figure the old walrus arranged the job himself and then tried to put the blame on me to keep me away from Abigail."

"A nasty old bird. But you could always elope. She could buy an island with her earrings."

"It's on the table. I'd say Christmas would be a perfect time to pop the question, what with my book coming out. She even mentioned throwing a big ball for me during the holidays."

"You sly rascal, Welles. How did you ever charm a goddess?"

"Skip it. Besides, I'm not sold on the ball idea. The last one was more trouble than it was worth."

"Yes, I remember your telling me. And this Matthewson person, any more encounters with him?"

"No, but there will be if he runs more of those hit pieces. And this time, I won't stop with breaking his nose."

"Now, there, Welles, be prudent. A journalist is among the lowest orders of men. They exist only to deceive and sow discord, because they are thoroughly depraved and degenerate. It would be foolish for you to bring further attention to yourself in that way, however much that rat deserves such blows."

"I feel like giving it to him anyway," I snarled. "A nice, thorough beatdown. That's the only way of getting any justice in this crooked world."

"Vengeance is seldom justice, Welles," Nigel said gravely. "By recompensing Matthewson for what he does to you, are you not lowering yourself to his sordid level? Retaliation may be satisfying in the moment you enact it, but scarcely afterward. I think, should you go forward with your plan of pummeling the journalist vermin, you would receive a rather empty sensation. No, Welles, I don't advise it. Vouch for your innocence and uprightness much as you can, but do not engage with such scum. You play their twisted, despicable game, much to their filthy delight, when you try to get back at them."

Our conversation drifted into more pleasurable topics, and the memory faded like mist in the morning sun. But its effect was strong upon me. Walloping weasels like Matt Duryea wouldn't bring Nigel back, and it wouldn't help me find out who had killed him, much less secure any real justice.

While I reflected on Nigel's sapience, Laura popped into my mind. The hazel eyes. The gentle cheeks. The luscious lips.

What's more, she was the only other person who cared about him, and she might know things that nobody else did, or cared to tell me. I hoped she had some of the pieces to the puzzle, but, besides that, I felt bad for the girl. Anybody who meant that much to Nigel had to mean something to me.

A minute after I texted her with an invitation to lunch, she replied with her address and said I could come by when convenient. I headed to a cozy little house on Amherst Drive, just south of Marquette Avenue. Two stately Cottonwood trees towered over the sidewalk and flanked a gravel driveway that entered the property at an acute angle from the northeast. There was a little patch of lawn amidst the xeriscape and a flowerbed of roses beneath one of the windows. Everything was well kept and homely.

Laura wore a white blouse and sky blue jeans as tight as a cannibal's drum. In the daylight, her hair took on a heavenly luster, like polished ebony.

"Thanks for the invitation," I said, once I was inside the vestibule. Nigel's painting of the hillside was opposite his watercolor of the river.

"He always wanted me to have them," Laura said. "They're beautiful, aren't they?"

I nodded, but not enough to dispel that irksome mist that was creeping over my eyes again. Laura put a gentle hand on my arm and smiled softly and conducted me through a series of bright rooms with bay windows, and lace curtains, and walls painted with gentle hues, and some old furniture that had been in the family for generations, and a shelf full of old vaudeville records and old plays. The place felt snug. A guy could get comfortable here.

We sat in a breakfast nook that was flooded with daylight and watched the sparrows flutter through the back garden. The white walls and gentle design of the kitchen smiled upon us in the solitude.

My intention had been to extract whatever information I could about Nigel, and learn why he had been so hesitant to tell me about her the last time I saw him, but something tugged at me to hold off because now wasn't the right time.

Instead, we spoke of our memories of him, and this, in turn, led to our discussing shared interests. Laura had a collection of Jane Austen's novels, each printed early last century, which prompted me to mention my collection of Shakespeare. Then, she wanted to know about my novels, why I liked writing, how long I had been doing it, where I got all my ideas. The conversation flowed delightfully from there.

I could have talked with her until the day of judgement, but she had rehearsals, so I left after two pleasant hours and made for Schuler's Shop. Some contrast between Laura's house and this rathole – a drab, soulless, stuccoed building in the sordid international district. The front windows had bars covered with more bars, and the front doors looked like they could encase a vault. I rang a slimy button and waited.

Across Central, a shirtless vagrant I could smell from here was dragging a club around and threatening anybody that got within a hundred feet of him. A guy pushing a shopping cart stopped, took his club out of the cart, and proceeded to battle the shirtless guy with it. Two crack addicts at a nearby bus stop applauded the scene with amusement.

Keys jangled into locks. A second door opened, then a narrow screen at the top of the first door.

"What do you want?" snarled a voice that sounded like it only ran on hard liquor.

"See Schuler."

"Why do you want to see Schuler?"

"It's about a jade."

"What jade?"

"Mighty nice jade of Bai Suzhen."

"Who?"

"Don't tell me you don't know who that is."

"This is an American store. What makes you think we've got that Chinese junk here?"

"The fact you know it's Chinese."

The voice rattled off a series of oaths and jangled more keys. The door that belonged in a vault whipped open, revealing a tall party, about forty-five, that didn't look as tough as that voice sounded. Not that he didn't try his best to look tough for a guy with arms like overcooked spaghetti noodles.

A bit of snot trickled down his left nostril and onto a brown mustache teeming with crumbs of food and an especially prominent bit of beef poking out of a gap in the hair like a mouse ready to come out of its hole. He wore a faded shirt of a bald eagle wearing a biker's jacket and riding a Harley Davidson over a chasm of flames, but his gut bulged the fabric so much the image practically looked three-dimensional. I decided not to ask him if he was with child.

A cheap linoleum floor was covered with clumps of dust and a few circular bulbs threw dingy, opaque light onto shelves filled with everything from crude toys and wrenches to bicycle parts and cans of paint. Why would Nigel take a rare jade to this dump?

The shop smelled like it had been embedded with the miasma of twenty unwashed armpits. I surmised the stench of this room was coming from two primary sources – the guy that had let me in, and the guy that stood behind the counter, Schuler. He looked old but cogent and smiled at me the way a toad smiles after it eats a fly. A few gray hairs clung fastidiously to his scalp, like an endangered species bracing for extinction. His eyes were sunken and sickly green, like two olives at the bottom of a jar that had expired six months ago. His chin was tilted to the right and looked like it had been stepped on by an elephant.

Schuler took a chubby pointer finger and steered it up to his nose, until he remembered I was watching him and had the finger take a detour to his ear instead. He poked it around a little while, settled on something, and pulled out a block of earwax as long as a birthday candle.

"If you pushed a wick in the middle," I remarked, "you might be able to put that up for sale."

"An innovative suggestion," Schuler ribbited as he set his wax to the side of the cash register and wiped his finger off on a white, collared shirt that had a dozen similar stains. "One must be resourceful to endure in this trade."

"A competitive business?"

"Highly. I evaluate each item offered me with the utmost circumspection. The slightest miscalculation can be baleful to my livelihood."

"How was your evaluation of the Bai Suzhen jade?"

"Ah," Schuler smiled while scratching under his left armpit. "The jade required an especially precise analysis which I reserve for singular occasions. As such, disclosure of further information concerning the jade is kept within the sacred circle of buyer, which was myself; seller, who shall remain unnamed; and witness, which was Clint."

Schuler said the last few words with a languid glance at the doorman with the runny nose.

"You'll make it the sacred quadrilateral," I said as I reached into my pocket and dangled some dough below Schuler's nose. When his long, dirty fingernails reached for the cash, I tucked it into my pocket.

"You'll get it if you answer my questions. Who sold you the jade?"

Schuler stared hard at me with those olives. They looked like they were being brought to a boil and about to burst.

"Don't do it, George," Clint admonished as another stream of snot rolled out of his nostril. "Don't tell him anything."

"I already know you've got it because your doorman let it slip," I smirked. "Get to talking."

"You must remember to be more watchful with your words, Clint. Information is a precious resource, particularly in this trade."

"Don't be telling this jerk," Clint snapped vehemently enough that a few of the crumbs popped out of his mustache and plummeted to the ground.

"Be quiet, Clint, and sit down."

Clint scowled and stomped over to a dirty stool by the window. More snot dripped out of his nose.

"I must first have your name for my records," Schuler pulled a binder out from a desk behind him and placed it delicately on the counter.

"The Count of Monte Cristo."

"Very well," Schuler smirked as he scribbled on the greasy page just beside an unsightly yellow smear. His handwriting would make a doctor blush.

"Now let's have it," I snapped.

“Nigel Wilfred brought the jade in,” Schuler said. “I conducted my evaluation, calculated the magnitude of risk I would take on by purchasing the item, and negotiated. We reached an agreement swiftly.”

“Who came with him?”

“Nigel Wilfred was alone.”

“How much did he sell it for?”

Schuler picked his nose, chuckled, and said, “Is it really necessary for you to know?”

“How much did he sell it for?”

"I never disclose what I receive in private trade," Schuler smirked while scratching at his rear. "However, I can assure you the sum provided was more than sufficient for such."

"Where's the jade now?"

Schuler sighed placidly and folded his arms. The grease on his neck shined.

"Where's the jade now?"

"Clint, the gentleman is becoming a nuisance."

"Don't ask me to get involved with this," Clint sniveled and folded his noodle arms and spat against the window. The saliva trickled slowly, like condensation on the side of a cold soda can.

"Whatever amount you planned on giving me would not be sufficient to outweigh the value of living," Schuler said. "What you have learned is all the information I will provide. Now, unless you have interest in my collection, or have a specimen of your own to offer, I request you recompense me suitably and leave."

I slid Schuler's coin across the counter and left. Across Central, a porky cop was giving the shirtless vagrant I could smell from here a heavy taze. The guy with the shopping chart and the two crack addicts at the bus stop applauded the gesture heartily.

Schuler's relative silence was reason enough for suspicion without wondering why Nigel would take the jade there, of all places. For that matter, why would he take it anywhere? Why wouldn't he just give it to Bigelow so he would display his paintings? That was Nigel's motivation for stealing the jade in the first place, wasn't it? And if he had sold the jade, why would he bother asking Brody for dough?

12

LAURA

If Nigel had really sold Schuler the jade, that would keep Bigelow the prohibitive favorite for arranging his demise. After all, Brody and his smurf sidekick both claimed Nigel had been running away from rough guys, and rough guys Bigelow had in no short supply. It wasn't difficult to imagine him sending Neville after Nigel when it became apparent Nigel wasn't going to be holding up his end of the agreement.

But that was assuming Schuler was telling the truth, which didn't seem wise. If Nigel had sold the jade for anything close to its worth, he wouldn't have needed to drop by Brody's to ask for dough. Somebody was lying; maybe they all were.

While I listened to Dvorak's *Symphony From The New World* that evening, I thought of the haunts Nigel and I frequented while we mused on life and love. We had wondered what things would look like when we came of age and established ourselves in the world, what we would drive, where we would live, how we would dress, how many girls would seek our attention. I recalled Nigel's prophecy that I would be more famous than he.

In a way, he was right. In every way, I wished he were around to tell me as much.

I texted Laura the next morning and arranged to take her out to dinner that night. A cozy little nook in Nob Hill was my go to spot whenever I wanted a mirthful experience, and I figured the vivacity of the place would do her good. She seemed to think so, too, because she replied the moment I sent the text with as palpable eagerness as a text message could convey.

In a white skirt and a gentle blouse that combined magenta and violet in an agreeable way, Laura was as comely as ever. She wasn't as down as she had been that night at Bigelow's, or even yesterday, but Nigel's death still bothered her. What else could you expect?

"So, you brought some nice company with you tonight, huh, Dickens?" growled Ruth, the middle-aged lady who owned the joint. "About time."

"How goes it, Ruth?"

"Same old grind, same old customers, same old place. What's got into you, Dickens? Why'd you decide to start living sensibly and going out with pretty girls?"

"It must be something in the air."

"Well, I hope it stays there. You know what a fella like you needs? A wife. How old is she?"

"Twenty-two."

"One year younger than you. And mighty pretty."

"Thank you, ma'am," Laura said.

"And mighty polite," Ruth raised her eyebrows. "Better hold on to this one, Dickens."

There was no sense in discussing Nigel immediately, so I let the conversation take its natural course. When it began to ebb, I gently broached the topic.

"Nigel was always open about anything that interested him, but he wouldn't tell me much about you. Any idea why he'd be so secretive?"

"No," she said, the mere mention of his name drawing a rueful expression from her angelic face. "People often saw us together, especially when he took me out to eat."

"How'd he get along with Bigelow?"

"Nigel was always polite. I think he would have been so, even if he didn't want his paintings to be displayed. But Whit hated him. He'd never gotten over our breakup, and was jealous of me and Nigel. At first, Nigel didn't seem to be bothered by it, but I think the tension troubled him over time."

"Then why didn't he try somewhere else?"

Laura paused, bit her lip, and looked down at the floor.

"Whit practically controls the Albuquerque art trade. If Nigel had spurned him, nobody would accept his artwork because Whit would threaten them if they did. Besides, Nigel knew what reach Whit has. If he displayed even one of his paintings, that would have established him internationally."

That didn't make sense, since the Italian barkeep said Nigel had to beg Bigelow to even consider displaying his art, but I put that aside for the time being. I told her about Murdoch and the incongruities of Nigel driving a Porsche and affording those appointments while squeaking by on a busboy's income.

"Whit usually drives a Porsche," she replied. "He must have let Nigel use it. It could have been about the..."

"Jade?"

She lowered her eyes and nodded.

"Did Nigel really steal it?"

Laura hesitated a long time before answering, "Yes."

"I thought you didn't know anything about it," I frowned.

"I'm sorry, I should have told you the other night, but I didn't want anybody to overhear us. I never saw the jade, but he told me he had it. You see, Nigel and I were going to run away together, and he wanted enough money to get us wherever we wanted to go. He sold the jade the morning before he died. We intended to leave after my performance that night, but I was afraid it wasn't going to work. I was afraid something was going to happen, as I mentioned before, especially once Nigel told me Whit was having him followed. I tried to warn him, but he didn't think Whit would act so quickly. He thought he had more time."

A tear that had been welling up in her eye for the duration of her monologue slowly trickled down her cheek. She wiped it away gently.

"If you were afraid, why didn't you just call the whole thing off?"

"Oh, I tried to tell Nigel, but he wouldn't listen. He didn't expect everything to happen so fast."

How did she know everything happened fast?

"What about Murdoch? Think he had anything to do with it?"

"I don't know," she shook her head sadly. "Nigel never talked about him."

"He ever talk about Murdoch's wife?"

A look of disdain spread across Laura's face. "He did."

"Like her much?"

“Not particularly. She’s a very nasty person.”

“I don’t know. She seemed pleasant to me.”

“Of course. She always acts that way at first. Especially to men she wants to manipulate.”

“So you know her?”

“Unfortunately, yes. I’ve seen her at The Parthenon many times. She even spoke to me on a few occasions, just to be a snob. She always entered the back way, because she would come out of Whit’s office. They must have been carrying on.”

“Then why was Bigelow jealous of you?” I frowned.

“Whit always wanted me, even from the beginning. Just because he sees her doesn’t mean he still doesn’t want me.”

“What’d Nigel have to do with her?”

"If she had her way, she would have been seeing him instead of Whit. But he wouldn’t see her. That’s why she told Whit to kill him. That’s why she told Whit he had the jade. Nobody else could have known about it, except her. She may have even helped Nigel get the jade just so she could provoke Whit into killing him.”

“She wouldn't have to do that, if Bigelow already hated Nigel’s guts.”

"Whit wouldn't have Nigel killed simply out of spite, so long as he was helping him get the jade. But once she told him Nigel had it, Whit wasn't going to wait. That was just the way she wanted it, because if she couldn't have Nigel, then neither could anybody else. If it hadn't been for *her*, none of this would have happened."

I wasn't entirely convinced about that theory, but there wasn't much more to say, so I directed the conversation to the scrumptious meal before us, and the pleasant discourse we had enjoyed before I asked about Nigel resumed.

"How do you like Dickens, miss?" Ruth asked Laura when we were finishing.

"I think he's a gentleman.

"You do, huh? He must be on his best behavior tonight. Last time he was in here, he told off a couple of Walt Whitman fans because he didn't like their views on poetry."

"Really?" Laura looked at me with mischievous disapproval.

I shrugged. "Free verse is garbage."

"One of them even offered me forty dollars to poison the man," Ruth continued. "Forty dollars!"

"Will you do it?" Laura asked.

"I'm holding out for fifty," Ruth replied with a wry smile.

I took Laura home. I had to park several blocks away because somebody on Amherst was having a party and every square inch of curb space was filled. But the walk to her house was pleasant, what with the lady at my elbow and the serene curtain of sky overhead.

In her living room, a series of porcelain figurines of geishas stood next to the clock on the mantle, and a tapestry of an idyllic Oriental meadow hung from one of the walls. Why hadn't I noticed them yesterday?

"Where'd you get these things?" I asked.

"Whit has no use for some of his goods. Maybe he thought giving them to me would make me more interested in him. Maybe he thought I would like them."

"The sap."

"They are very rare, though," Laura walked to the mantle and took a figurine in her hands. "They might be worth ten thousand each on the open market."

I whistled in surprise and nodded at the tapestry. "Same with that thing?"

"Yes," she said, moving her fingers across its surface. "Whit told me this kind usually sells for fifty thousand."

"I found a Zhongshan suit in Nigel's closet. Ever seen him in one before?"

"Never."

"Think he swiped it off Murdoch for spite?"

"I don't think so. Maybe *she* gave it to him."

"Amelia?"

Laura nodded silently. The very mention of that woman made her cheeks blush, but quick. Not that I blamed her. A dish like Amelia trying to pry Nigel away would be plenty reason enough for rage, even if she didn't have anything to do with Bigelow bumping him off.

13

BRUTE FORCE

As soon as I had bid Laura good evening, the vanity of my mission presented itself to me. What did I expect to find that would be of any consequence to anyone, especially myself? Nigel was gone; there was no bringing him back. Even if I had put the finger on Bigelow, or Amelia, and put together enough evidence to send them both to the chair, Bigelow had the law in one pocket and the media in the other. There was no "justice" to be had in a situation like that.

So Bigelow was behind it. Or Amelia. Or both. So Nigel had stolen a jade and sold it, or hid it instead. What difference did any of it make? My friend was perished, and nothing in this world could be done to change that rueful reality.

As I ruminated on the hopelessness of my endeavor, the disquieting sound of distant footsteps reached my ears. A dark outline of a shape moved half a block behind me. When I made a right on the street where I had parked, so did the footsteps. I was being followed.

While the shape gained on me from the back, another unfriendly bulk moved toward me from the other direction. Then it slipped into the shadows, and the guy behind me began speedwalking until fewer than ten feet separated us. I sprinted to outgain him significantly, until a foot poked out from behind a tree and sent me onto my stomach.

A hand emerged from the darkness and snatched me off the ground like a metal claw grabs a prize in an arcade game. The other hand balled up into a fist as big as a watermelon and pounded my chin with such force I sailed into bushes twenty feet back of the sidewalk.

Enormous fingers were plunged into the bush, grabbed my shirt like they were crumpling a piece of paper, and yanked me out. By this time, the other guy had arrived, and promptly kicked my stomach with a foot that looked like it used a size twenty shoe.

"You know, I read some before, chum," said the voice that came with the hands, as it lit a match and blew on a cigarette. "Read a guy called Tolstoy. You heard of the mug?"

"Sure," was all I could manage to say.

"I don't like what I read. Too many words. Too many characters. That's the kind of stuff that ties a guy's brain into pretzels."

"I didn't know you had a brain."

Another smack followed. The cigarette compared to those fingers like a thumbtack compared to a bunch of bananas.

"They say he's called Welles," the voice that came with the feet said, "but I don't think that's an appropriate name. What do you say, Mitts?"

"Sure, Feet," Mitts sneered. "Suppose we calls him Tolstoy, on account of the crack he made?"

"Suppose we does," Feet snickered.

"Suppose you let us have your car keys, Tolstoy," Mitts said. "We wanna take you somewheres."

"Suppose you hand 'em over, Tolstoy," Feet seconded. "We got plans on giving you a nice evening."

Mitts gave me a "gentle" slap that only knocked me onto my back. When I rolled to the side in dazed noncompliance, he pulled the keys out of my pocket and flipped them to Feet.

"Start her, huh, Feet?"

Then, he lugged me to the car and shoved me into the back like I was a piece of luggage. Once his bulky frame sat next to me, Feet slowly drove off.

"Where we going?" I mumbled, when some of the pain had begun to subside.

"Did you hear that, Feet?" Mitts sneered. "Tolstoy wants to know where we're going."

"Sure he do," Feet snickered. "All them artist types are just bursting with curiosity, ain't they?"

"You're Bigelow's goons."

"Did you hear that, Feet?" Mitts said. "Tolstoy thinks we're with Bigelow."

"Ain't he a bright one," Feet chortled.

Mitts gave me a casual elbow that felt like getting kicked by a brontosaurus.

"We don't like to see guys doing things that ain't smart, Tolstoy," Mitts remarked. "You're doing things that ain't smart."

"That how you figure it?"

"Did you hear that, Feet? Tolstoy wants to know if that's how I figure it."

"Better show him how you figure it," Feet suggested with a snort.

"That's a good idea. We're gonna teach you a lesson, chum. A lesson that'll does you a lot of good."

"Aren't you thoughtful."

"Did you heart that, Feet?" Mitts snickered. "Tolstoy thinks we're thoughtful."

"Give him props for the manners," Feet snickered.

"Yeah. Here's your props for the manners," Mitts said as Feet stopped in an empty elementary school parking lot. Mitts hurled me out onto the asphalt and beat me like a punching bag for the next five minutes. Feet added the occasional kick for fun.

"That's a little tip on advising you not to keep looking into this Wilfred matter," Mitts informed me as he lit another cigarette and cooled the match by pressing it into my cheek. "You been busy sticking your nose places it ain't supposed to be going. We don't think that's so good. We don't think that's so smart. What's more, Eyebrows don't think that's so smart."

"Who?"

"Eyebrows Da Silva. He wanted us to take you this message. We think you better listen to it good."

"Who cares what you think," I barely had the strength to say.

"Did you hear that, Feet?" Mitts snickered. "Tolstoy don't care what we think."

"Impudent, for a guy in his position," Feet snorted.

Mitts poked my keys between his fingers, balled up another fist, and landed a blow that felt like getting hit by a morning star.

"You might need these, chum," he sneered as he opened the hand and dropped the keys on my swollen chin. Then, he and his pal lumbered off into the night, but not before adding a farewell blow that knocked me out cold.

14

A DANGEROUS PROFESSION

After a while, I came out of it. I didn't know how long it took, but it didn't seem long. Ten minutes, max, but more like five minutes.

Five minutes. You can do a lot of things in five minutes. You can fry an egg, swat a fly, tie your shoes, peel an orange, score a steak. In five minutes you can be shot, stabbed, thrown out a window, run over by a tractor, attacked by a swarm of bats.

Five minutes. A short nap. A pleasant slumber. A brief reprieve from the world and the flesh and the devil. Refreshed much, Welles?

It was a struggle to open my eyes, let alone think about trying to get up and drive away. When I was finally able to move my head, I glanced at my car. It was standing still, like a horse waiting for its rider.

"Brother, you're gonna be there a while," I grunted.

The stars smirked down at me. More time passed. Doubtless, bruises were already forming. Big, ugly bruises as wide as hotcakes and as black as the darkest night. I felt like a half-eaten pigeon.

When the pain had stopped enough I could start to hear myself think, I realized laying on asphalt wasn't the most efficient way of administering first aid. So, I pushed my limbs around, turned onto my stomach, and crawled to the car.

Eventually, I was in the driver's seat and turning the ignition. I guess I was all right. My head throbbed every time I moved it, and my body felt like it had been trampled by a herd of mammoths, but I guess I was all right.

I went to a small ER off Lomas. In the waiting room, a desk was fronted by glass that looked like it could stop a cannon. I rang the little red bell beside the glass and summoned a chick with fake eyelashes as long as matches. She gave me a disgusted look and turned up her nose and snorted and started typing at a computer.

"That bad, huh?" I said.

"What's your name?" she growled into a speaker taped to the glass.

"Preston Welles."

"What happened to you?"

"A piano fell out of the sky and landed on me."

"Any internal bleeding?"

"That's what I came here to find out."

"Do you get these injuries frequently?"

"Depends on the company I keep."

The chick curled her lip, folded her chubby arms, leaned back in the chair, and gave me a long, hard glare.

"I don't like your attitude."

"I don't like my attitude, either. It's sordid and odious and vile and abominable and fiendish. I spend all my evenings weeping over it. Now, will you be a good girl scout and get me somebody that can do something besides make me repeat things aloud that I already know?"

She shut off the speaker and snarled something into a corded phone. While she did, I looked over the waiting room. Nobody else was in here but a serious, middle-aged man sitting across from the glass.

The serious man wore a silver, North Ridge turtleneck that reached his chin and made his head look like it was floating in space. He had a small bandage across the bridge of his nose and two penetrating blue eyes with which he was exploring my face.

"Hideous, isn't it?" I said.

The serious man with the bandage on his nose snorted in repulsion and looked down at his phone, which was tilted so I could see the stock market on the screen. He stared at the screen, then at me, then up at the ceiling as he mechanically shook his head. The Dow Jones must have gone down one-tenth of a percent.

"What are you in for, Mac?"

The serious man glared at me and went back to the phone without a word. Now, he opened the *Washington Post* app and read a long, tedious article about an election in a distant banana republic and what its results would mean for the future of "democracy." Then, he began playing an "election update" video featuring a man with a British accent who sounded like he'd be better suited narrating a National Geographic nature show.

"Hey, you," a gruff voice snarled through the speaker. "The doctor will see you now."

"Me?"

The chick snorted again. She had that trick down to perfection. She should consider trying out on a talent show. Then, she tramped over to the door, slapped a big red button, and folded her arms as I stumbled through the doorway. I followed her past a row of computers and across a hallway into an examination room on the first left.

“Here you go,” she growled. She snorted again, slammed the door, and waddled down the hall. What a gal.

I didn't like the lights; they were cold and vengeful and belonged in an interrogation room. The walls were beige, and so was the tile. A clock that looked like it was about to stop was suspended to the top of the adjacent wall by a string that looked like it was about to snap. The seconds hand creaked across the face, like an old car that didn’t want to start.

The wall opposite me had a cabinet and a sink and a counter with paper towels and boxes of latex gloves and a tray of syringes and needles and other nasty things wrapped in nice paper sheets. Maybe they thought that wrapping them like they were candy made them more appealing to kids. The mirror was suspended above the sink, but I didn’t bother looking in it. I figured the effect would have been something like Dorian Gray seeing his portrait after it had decayed.

The wall on my right had a chart with an anatomy of the human body, down to the last square inch of the tip of the toenail, with labels made of faint little words that couldn’t be read without a microscope. Flanking this chart were pictures of kids dressed like adults and making cutesy poses that made anyone with taste gag.

After a few minutes, the doctor appeared and scowled at me through black-rimmed glasses and then scowled at his clipboard. He couldn't have been more than thirty-five; had thick, brown hair; and a pair of thick ears that stuck out of the sides of his head, like stop signs on a school bus. He wore blue scrubs and brown hiking shoes that looked like they weighed twenty pounds each.

"You're Preston Welles?" he asked with a voice that sounded like it thought it was pretty good.

"I'm Preston Welles."

"Do you feel fine, Mr. Welles?"

"Like a newborn baby."

He glared at me, and then glared at the clipboard. He motioned toward the examination chair.

"Hop up there and we'll look you over. How did you sustain your injuries?"

"I was walking to my car when a guy as big as a bus decided to pick me up."

"He picked you up?" the doctor scowled.

"Uh-huh. I guess I can get real cute occasionally. Then, he started smacking me from one sidewalk to another. His pal joined in on the act with a kick from time to time."

He snorted at me, then snorted at the clipboard. What did the clipboard ever do to him?

The doctor set the clipboard he didn't like on the counter, washed his hands for five minutes, dried them off with fifty paper towels, and strapped two gloves on each hand.

"You may have sustained some serious injuries," he stared intently at me.

"Think so?"

He glared at me, then glared at the clipboard. "What is your pain on a scale of one to ten, Mr. Welles?"

"Eight and a half, over under."

"Can you raise your arms?"

"Sure, only it feels like my shoulders are being crushed by a tank when I do."

The doctor snorted at me, then snorted at the clipboard. He poked around at my shoulders and back and chest and arms and neck for a little while.

"I recommend we analyze your entire body," he concluded. "The machine room is down the hall."

I went to the machine room down the hall, where a contraption that looked like something from *The Matrix* was sitting.

“Lay down inside this,” the chick that snorted ordered.

I stumbled into the machine and laid down on a cushion with a sheet and a pillow. I felt like I was in a pod being sent to space. There was a rumbling noise, then a spinning noise like a washing machine operating. Eventually, all the noises stopped, and the chick opened the machine. From somewhere distant came the sound of a printer running and spitting out papers.

"Go back to the examination room,” she snarled.

“Can’t we do it here? This is much more comfortable.”

When I finally got back to the examination room, the doctor was leaning against the counter, putting the results onto the clipboard. He read them in several minutes of silence and set the clipboard down.

“You don’t have any broken bones or internal injuries,” he muttered, almost like he was disappointed. “Everything is intact. Do you exercise often?”

“I hit baseballs and lift weights.”

"And is your profession taxing?"

"No, but it's dangerous."

"How so?"

"I tend to get my brains beat out."

“Obviously a result of your idiocy," the doctor sneered. "Don’t do anything for a week or two. Your body needs time to recover from the trauma it endured. I recommend you get as much sleep as you can. If the pain is overwhelming, I can write you a prescription for something, but don’t take it if you’re going to be driving because it will make you drowsy. Be sure to get plenty of fluids. The body requires water for repair.”

The doctor glared at me, then glared at the clipboard.

“One other thing. You’ve been reported to the state health department for suspicions of insanity. When was your most recent mental health evaluation?”

“Huh? Who reported me?”

“Chandler Murdoch,” the doctor replied like he was saying the name of a god. “Is he your primary healthcare provider?”

“I’ve only seen him once, and he didn’t evaluate me.”

The doctor frowned at me, then frowned at the clipboard. “That means your symptoms must be apparent enough to be detected without evaluation. How are you feeling, mentally? Do you seem stable?”

“I feel like Muhammed Ali used my brains for a punching bag.”

The doctor snorted at me, then snorted at the clipboard.

"We operate under the three strikes system. A patient reported for suspicions of insanity three times can be institutionalized if the district attorney petitions for it, which seems likely in your case since Dr. Murdoch is very close with the district attorney. I strongly suggest you seek mental health care immediately. Dr. Murdoch is the best psychiatrist in the state, possibly in the country. You should see him regularly."

"I don't like that idea."

"How do you like the idea of being institutionalized?" the doctor snarled. "Does that suit you better?"

"Neither option suits me better. I saw Murdoch because I suspect he was involved in the death of my friend. That's why he reported me."

"Nonsense," the doctor snorted. "Dr. Murdoch would never harm anyone or anything."

"I have a hard time believing that."

The doctor scowled at me, then scowled at the clipboard.

"You'd be wise to listen to my advice, Mr. Welles," he said through his teeth. Then, he grabbed the clipboard he liked glaring and glowering and scowling and snorting at and left. I got off the examination chair, went down the same hallway, went by the computers and the chick that snorted and went out the door.

15

ACT OF VIOLENCE

By the time I got home, it was almost dawn. I went straight to bed and stayed there until the afternoon, when I awoke as refreshed as a guy can be after getting the stuffings beaten out of him. My body felt usable enough for me to get around normally, and my head felt clear enough to think at normal speed.

I had assumed, as much as I could assume after those two brutes had finished with me, that Bigelow had them tail me and send me the message. After all, he was the one who wanted the jade in the first place.

But hearing Murdoch reported me for being a nut changed my mind. Maybe it wasn't Bigelow's work. Maybe Murdoch had more to do with it than he pretended and knew more than he pretended to know. Maybe, just maybe, the two (with Amelia's help, if Laura was to be believed) worked together to kill Nigel, and were tying up loose ends by having me smacked around and listed as a crackpot.

And what of Laura? It was suspicious those thugs had knocked me around right after I'd spent the evening with her. Sure, it was possible Bigelow was having me followed out of fear of what I'd find out, or jealousy over Laura, or both. But if that were the case, why didn't those mugs say he'd sent them? And if Bigelow's jealousy had motivated the message, why didn't they tell me to stay away from Laura?

Yes, Laura. Maybe she wouldn't answer her dressing room door that night because she wasn't in there. Maybe she was out contributing to Nigel's demise.

But why would she do that when he was so in love with her? Her, a killer? Her, with the hazel eyes, the gentle cheeks, the luscious lips? I couldn't come to that conclusion now.

I tossed an apple up and down for several minutes, only I didn't scowl or snort or glare or glower at it. Only clipboards deserved that treatment. Clipboards were the scourge of society.

Another knock at the door. More cops? More brutes? More psychiatrists?

I was wrong. I was glad to be wrong. It was special delivery of an ornately embellished cream envelope with exquisite handwriting of my name and address came that afternoon. The stamp depicted a pagoda overlooking a marshy lake, with several trees and a snow-topped mountain peak towering in the background.

Inside was a glossy sheet of paper with the following printed in hard ink:

Mrs. Murdoch requests your attendance on June 18th at 7 p.m. for a traditional Chinese performance at Chandler Murdoch's residence. Please R.S.V.P.

That was tomorrow evening. Not much time for R.S.V.P., but what did I care about that? A golden opportunity to look through Murdoch's realm had just been served up on a platter. I had designs on searching every square inch of the place, and I figured the quack wasn't liable to like what I found.

Was it a trap? Possibly. But I'd had it in mind to pay Murdoch another visit, and there was no time like the present.

I was content to spend the rest of the day refreshing myself after my playdate with those bruisers. But then I thought more of Laura. If I hadn't been beaten to a pulp, I probably would have spent all night thinking of her. Until I found real evidence she was involved, I wanted to let her in on what I'd found out.

So, against my better judgement, I went back to The Parthenon. Approaching it still made me feel like I had taken a time machine back to classical antiquity.

"So you came back, huh?" the slender doorman in the tuxedo sneered. "You must not listen very well. Or do you just like getting the fly swatter treatment?"

"I've got a few words for Bigelow."

"I'm sure you do," he snorted as he tapped the iPad and opened the wooden doors. "But don't say I didn't warn you."

Laura was at the piano, just as she had been previously. Tonight, she was playing Liszt's *Liebestraume No. 3.*

"Do you take tips, miss?" I asked.

"Preston!" she said in surprise, briefly pausing her play. "What happened to your face? Are you feeling all right? What are you doing here?"

"Just calling on a girl. You wouldn't happen to have seen her around, would you?"

"What does she look like?" she smiled as she resumed playing.

"Oh, very beautiful. Ebony hair like black silk. Hazel eyes that make a guy's legs wobbly when he's sitting down. Pearl teeth. Exquisite figure."

Laura giggled and said, "I don't know who you're referring to."

"I took her out to dinner last night," I continued, leaning against the piano and tapping my fingers on the side of it to match her play. "We had a delightful time."

"What happened next?"

"It was getting late, so I took her home. Only thing was, on the walk back to my car, a couple of fists and feet fell on me. That makes it hard for a guy to get around."

"What?"

"Two brutes named Feet and Mitts gave me the works. They said Eyebrows Da Silva sent them and told me to quit looking into Nigel. Ever heard of those characters before?"

"Of course not. Why would I?" She seemed insulted at the thought of being familiar with their company.

"They never came around here, for instance?"

"I never heard those names, but it's possible. They could have come through the back door, like that *woman* does."

"Bigelow ever mention this Eyebrows Da Silva party?"

"Not to me."

"I'm wondering if that's Bigelow's nickname."

"I can't tell you much about it, Preston. I try not to talk to Whit when I can avoid it."

"That makes sense. But I'm getting off topic. I was telling you about my night with that fine lady and what happened after I bid her good night."

"Yes," Laura smiled. "You were."

"As I was saying, that roughhousing treatment can make it difficult on a guy. So I went to the E.R. just to get checked out."

"Was anything broken?"

"Not even my shoelaces. But what's more, I found out while I was in there I'm insane."

"You what?" Laura frowned.

"That creep Murdoch reported me for insanity. The E.R. doc said if I get two more strikes, I'm out and the D.A. can petition for them to put me in the looney bin."

"You can't be serious?"

"I tend to be. A bright future, isn't it?"

"Why would he do that to you? Did you threaten him?"

"My existence is a threat to him. You see, I don't have an enlightened soul."

"Don't be ridiculous. Aren't you curious why he would do that?"

“It isn’t that hard to figure out. He’s afraid I might find out how he contributed to Nigel’s death.”

“I don’t think so. Nigel went there because, because *she* wanted him to.”

I wondered how Laura knew this, since she claimed Nigel had never mentioned Murdoch.

“She? You mean Amelia?”

“Yes,” Laura said through her teeth. “I wouldn’t be surprised if she told Murdoch to report you for insanity, because she’s afraid you might find out how much she had to do with it all.”

“I would. Besides, she just sent me an invitation to a ‘traditional Chinese performance’ at Murdoch’s tomorrow night. I intend to accept.”

“You do? Oh, be careful. You don’t know what they have in mind.”

"It can't be any worse than what I got last night."

Laura finished her piece to hearty applause. Bigelow had come out of his office and was leaning on the rail, watching us.

“Did Bigelow ask you about me?” I asked.

“He asked if I talked to you. I said yes, but didn’t specify.”

“He didn’t want you to specify?”

"He got a call. It was good timing for me."

"Maybe he'll get a call this time," I said as Bigelow came down the stairs and toward us.

"I heard him tell Neville something about a package earlier," Laura whisphered. "He wanted it put in the safe."

"The jade?"

"I'm not sure. Here he comes now."

"I see you have returned, Mr. Welles," Bigelow said with the voice that sounded like biting into a fresh apple. "Laura told me you sought her out last time also. Is there any particular reason for this?"

"Suppose you figure out it's none of your business."

"Suppose you start minding your manners while you're in my place of business."

"Suppose you stop calling this racket a 'place of business'."

"Suppose I have Neville give you a lesson in etiquette."

"It wouldn't do any good. I'm a recalcitrant learner."

"So I see."

Bigelow turned to Laura.

"You played beautifully tonight, Laura, but it would be a shame to tarnish your reputation by continually associating with men like Mr. Welles. The Ambersons are dining here this evening. Let's tell them hello."

"Goodbye, Preston," Laura said, with her eyes lowered.

"I'll be escorting Laura to that table on the other side of the room," Bigelow said coldly as he took her arm. "I'd better not see you here when I return."

They disappeared into the crowd, and I glanced up at Bigelow's office door. If the jade was up there, I was going to find it.

Bigelow had left the lamp on and the curtains open. As the cityscape glowed brightly through the panes, I started with the desk. Then I went through each of his drawers, then poked around the bookshelves for secret compartments and hidden switches and all of the things bookshelves in movies have.

Bigelow's chair didn't have the jade, and neither did the paintings. But *The Death of Socrates* wasn't hanging on the wall like the other painting – it was fastened onto it. I tugged gently at the frame and the wall panel swung outward to reveal an open safe.

Bigelow's lamp was too dim to illuminate the inside of the safe, so I flicked on my phone's flashlight. There was an outer compartment, which had cash and a few folders, and an inner compartment with five combination locks that would take a week to open. I reached for one of the folders just as something sturdy struck the back of my head.

I slowly opened my eyes to Neville's mug sneering down at me. When the rest of the room came into focus, Bigelow was standing by his desk with his hands in his pockets.

"He's coming out of it," Neville observed with a sneer.

"Persistence is commendable, Mr. Welles," Bigelow said. "The great men of ages past would not be known to the modern world without it. What did you hope to find in my safe?"

"The jade."

"Ah, yes, the jade. I should like to know where the jade is."

"I should like to know, too," I muttered. "That's why you smacked me."

"I didn't smack you, Mr. Welles; Neville did. Brutality is an unbecoming quality which I never employ for any purpose. But Neville is entirely different. He rather enjoys the sensation of inflicting pain. Perhaps there is some deviant impulse within his mind that urges him to barbarism, even when it would be more efficient to pursue less violent alternatives. Had I come upon you looking into my safe, I would not have struck you from behind. I would have asked you to sit down, offered you some brandy, and discussed your motives for entering my office in the manner you did."

"That's good to know," I snorted as I slowly sat up. His floor didn't feel much better than that parking lot from last night.

"As I was saying," Bigelow resumed, "I never resort to brutality to extract information, but Neville is not as refined. If he desires to learn something, he uses his fists first and his mind – small as it may be – second. Why not spare yourself the trouble of dealing with a psychopathic brute and tell me where the jade is? I assure you there are more benefits to doing so than simply avoiding his savagery."

"I'll tell you where the jade is," I pointed at the safe. "Right in there."

Bigelow smiled and put his hands behind his back. "Simple logic should tell you I would have no reason to ask you where the jade was, and to search Wilfred's room, if I had it in my safe. Where is it?"

"I don't have it."

"This is your final opportunity, Mr. Welles. Either you will tell me where the jade is, or Neville will make you tell me where the jade is."

"If I knew where it is, I wouldn't be in here."

"I wish I could believe you," Bigelow lamented as he went to the door. "But trespassing must carry its own punishment."

"Where's the jade, twerp?" the meathead sneered as he pulled me to my feet.

"I don't have it."

"That isn't a satisfactory answer, twerp. Where's the jade?"

"I don't know."

Neville punched me into one of the bookshelves.

"There's nothing to gain by stalling, twerp. Just tell us where the jade is, and we'll let you go like this whole thing never happened."

"I don't know where the jade is."

Neville walked to Bigelow's desk, took out a small speaker, and tapped something on his phone. The first movement of Mozart's *Symphony No. 40 in G Minor* began to play.

"Do you like music, twerp? I like music. I like all kinds of music. But do you know what kind of music I really like, twerp? It's the sound of my fists hitting a guy's mug. Especially if it's a guy like you that thinks he's smart. Those are the best melodies."

This vicious cycle of smacks and cracks went on for several minutes. At least the meathead didn't hit as hard as Mitts. I didn't think anyone hit as hard as Mitts.

After a punch sent me over the desk, Bigelow opened the door.

"I don't like to see you in this state, Mr. Welles, but I warned you what would happen."

"You're Eyebrows Da Silva," I could barely get the words out. I didn't really think he was, but saying so was worth a try.

"Who?" Bigelow scowled like he'd never heard the name before.

"You're Eyebrows Da Silva."

"Who might that be?"

"Sent your mugs after me last night. Told me to quit looking into Nigel."

"The twerp's screwy," Neville snorted as he wiped his hands off with a towel.

"Anyone would be, after you were through with them," Bigelow said flatly. "I didn't send anyone to meet you last night, Mr. Welles. I had no intention of encountering you again, until you trespassed in my office. Presuming you do not make a habit of coming here, this will be our final encounter, and I am glad of it. If you were beaten by rough characters, as you claim, it was not done on my behalf. Howbeit, I recommend you stop your investigation before you get yourself killed. Nothing you find out will help Wilfred, anyway."

I wanted to take a poke at him, but I barely had enough strength to sit up. So I just grunted and rubbed what used to be the back of my head.

"Show Mr. Welles out the back way," Bigelow told the meathead. "It wouldn't be ideal for our customers to see him in this condition."

Beyond the back door was a circular flight of stairs. Neville shoved me down them with a sneer.

"Bon voyage, twerp."

I laid on the pavement and looked up at the building and the sky. This had to be getting close to a world record for beatdowns in a twenty-four-hour span.

After a few minutes, I lurched to where I had parked and drove home. I wouldn't have been this battered if I were a boxer.

16

GASLIGHT

From the murk of cruel mystery that personified the whole of this engagement, Duryea's sneering face reemerged. What was his angle? Why was he willing to tell me who hired him?

Clouds were building and a steady breeze was strengthening by the minute as Duryea's office came into view. Unusual, considering this is a desert that was experiencing a drought even by desert standards.

I parked in the same spot and stepped over the same collection of needles and trash and went inside. A guy was leaning against a wall made black by dirt, snickering and carrying out conversation with himself. He must have been one of those upstanding characters Duryea had mentioned.

"I went inside," the guy said. "He didn't want to see me. He told me to leave. Can you imagine? Him telling me to leave. You don't tell me to leave."

The guy snickered some more and began picking at his teeth with a hand that didn't look like it had been washed in a year.

"He was mad," he said maniacally, his eyes twinkling with wicked wonder. "He was real mad. But I got my way. I always get my way."

The guy said, with a much lower voice that made every hair on the back on my neck stand up, "You shouldn't be so forthcoming with it. Somebody might hear you. Then they'd know."

"Relax," the guy replied, now with the normal voice. "They won't know. They can't touch me. Not with two of us working together, they can't touch me."

"But the way you did it," the lower voice expostulated. "You just left him with the knife and all. They'll find your fingerprints. They'll get you."

"No, they won't," the normal voice smugly said. "I don't leave fingerprints. I don't leave clues. Don't try to make me nervous."

"I'm your friend. I don't want you to get a raw deal. You know what they're gonna do to you if they find out, don't you? Well, don't you?"

"Shut up," the normal voice muttered, the guy digging his nails into his arm.

"They're gonna take you back," the lower voice sang, in a taunting, depraved tone. "They're gonna put you back where you came from. They're gonna make sure you don't get away so easily this time."

"Shut up," the normal voice said, now a little louder. "Don't talk to me about that."

"They're gonna catch you, and they're gonna put you away again. You didn't like that, did you? You won't like that, will you?"

"Shut up," the normal voice said, almost to the point of shouting. "They're not going to get us. They're not going to take us back."

"You're right," the lower voice sneered. "They're not going to take *us* back. They're going to take *you* back. And they're not going to let you get away again."

"Shut up," the guy cocked back his head and roared. Now, the nails were so deep into his flesh I couldn't even see the cuticles. A crimson waterfall gushed down his arm.

He looked to the side abruptly. "You told them, didn't you?" his normal voice whispered. "You ratted on me."

"I would never do that. You should know better than to accuse me."

"You did it, you rat. Just like you did before. You've been against me from the beginning, haven't you? Answer me!"

With that, the guy ripped his hand out of his arm, formed a bloody fist, and swung a punch at his face. Before it could land, the other arm stopped it. He fell back against the wall, the arms struggling against each other.

"They won't get me," the normal voice grunted amidst the struggle. "I won't let them. You rat. You betrayed me again. I'll kill you."

The one arm overpowered the other arm in stopping the punch, and the guy flung himself onto the floor. He tried to punch himself again, only to be thwarted by the other arm. I'd seen enough.

Duryea was kicked back in the padded black chair, putting his shoes up on the desk and holding a shot glass with his right hand and a whiskey bottle with his left. That must have been his natural position.

"Greetings," he said with that toothy smirk. "What can I do for you?"

"You can start making sense. What's your angle?"

"My angle?" Duryea asked with a confused sneer.

"You know what I'm referring to. Start talking."

"You must mean the shamus business. A tough racket, that. When the cases aren't coming in, I live on a diet of whiskey and cigarettes. And look at the location. It gets me a sliver of mountains and two handfuls of hoodlums and homeless maniacs."

I reached across the desk and grabbed another handful of Duryea's collar. The sneer danced along his face, as insufferable as ever.

"Wait a minute, pal," Duryea tried to wriggle out of my grip. "If it's work you're after, I do it in spades. I'm not really tied down to anything at the moment. What's the job?"

I slammed him back into the chair. "Did Murdoch really hire you?"

"Murdoch?" Duryea frowned. "Who's Murdoch?"

"You know who he is."

"I've never worked for a Murdoch before, pal. You sure you aren't mistaken?"

"Then it was Amelia, wasn't it?"

"Amelia? Who's Amelia?"

"Listen, you," I snarled as I grabbed more collar. "I don't want any more doubletalk. Who really hired you, and why were you so eager to tell me in Brody's?"

"Brody's, huh? I saw you in Brody's?"

"You know you did."

Duryea rubbed his dimpled chin and threw another sneer my way. His eyes sparked with smug satisfaction.

"I think I know who you are," he said slowly. "You're Preston Welles. You're the guy who's pal bumped himself off."

"Stop playing dumb, Duryea. How are you tied up in all this?"

Duryea poured himself another drink. "Ahhhh," he sneeringly drawled. "That's fine whiskey. Care for some, Welles?"

"What did you have to do with it?"

"I wish I knew what you were referring to, Welles. I really do. It sounds like a fascinating ordeal. But quit acting like we know each other. You know as well as I do that we've never seen each other face to face in our lives."

"Oh yes, we have. I saw you at Brody's and then here."

"A great imagination," Duryea sneered. "It's good you have one, Welles, what with you being an artist and all. You must owe a lot to that mind of yours. But does it know the difference between reality and fiction?"

"Listen, you," I snarled.

"Oh, I wouldn't do that again if I was you, Welles. I happen to believe in the great American ideal of 'sue thy neighbor.' If you lay another finger on me, I'll press charges. As I recall, you have a bit of history with the coppers, don't you? It might not be so good for you to get their attention again, would it? Suppose you pretend you never came here today, just like you're pretending we know each other. Why not go home and take a nice, long nap? Maybe you'll start acting more sound. Maybe you'll stop behaving like a lunatic."

"I'm no lunatic."

"Oh, but you are, Welles. You're disturbed. That's why you should consider mental health treatment. I hear they can work wonders for maniacs like you. Better get started soon, or you might end up like that nut out in the hall. Then they'll put you away, but quick. You wouldn't want that, would you, Welles?"

"Murdoch told you to play dumb, didn't he?"

"Chandler Murdoch? There's an idea. You should see Chandler Murdoch for your imagination issues, Welles. They say he's the best psychiatrist in the state, possibly the country. Maybe then your nutty mind will stop making up things that never happened. That'd be good for both of us, wouldn't it, Welles?"

I looked at Duryea sitting there sneering at me until I couldn't take any more of it. Outside, the guy was back against the wall, still carrying on conversation, still pushing one arm against the other.

"You filthy rat," his usual voice snarled. "I'll kill you."

The struggle continued, and I went out the door. As I prepared to turn north on San Pedro, I wondered about Schuler's Shop. Why had Duryea wanted to steer me to that dump? I headed back to the international district.

The place looked as scummy and sordid as last time, only there weren't any shirtless vagrants across Central that I could smell from where I was. The narrow screen at the top of the first door slid open in response to my knock.

"What do you want?" snarled the voice that sounded like it only ran on hard liquor.

"See Schuler."

"Why do you want Schuler?"

"It's about a jade. Remember? You referred to it as 'Chinese junk'."

The voice rattled off more oaths and jangled more keys and the door that belonged in a vault whipped open. Clint scowled as snot trickled out of his nose. This time, he was wearing a shirt depicting Donald Trump riding an enormous bald eagle while heavenly faces of George Washington and Abraham Lincoln smiled approvingly in the background.

The place still smelled like it had been embedded with the miasma of twenty unwashed armpits. Schuler stood behind the counter and slowly pulled his left pointer finger out of his left nostril. His dirty fingernail was shining with yellow slime, so he slurped it up and wiped the finger off on another white, collared shirt with many such stains.

"Nigel never sold you the jade, did he?" I asked.

"Nigel?" Schuler's spread his lips widely, like a toad. "Who is Nigel?"

"Nigel Wilfred. I was in here two days ago asking you about him. Remember?"

"No, I'm afraid I don't," Schuler glanced at the doorman languidly. "Clint, do you remember seeing this gentleman before?"

Clint glared at me while more snot trickled out of his nose. "Course not," he snorted. "I'd remember seeing those fresh clothes if I had."

"What was the jade of?" Schuler asked me. I described it to him while he mined the other nostril.

"Ah, I would surely remember such a precious item. You must be mistaken. Are you a well man?"

"Don't try that," I snorted. "I was in here two days ago and both of you know it. Murdoch paid you off to play dumb, didn't he?"

"Murdoch?" Schuler squinted. "First you speak of a Nigel, and now you mention a Murdoch. I am afraid I do not know either of these persons, or yourself. You are imagining these things. A very sound imagination, to be sure, but not reflective of reality."

"I'm not imagining anything. Who paid you off?"

"Please calm yourself," Schuler sighed. "You seem to imply that somebody has paid me to pretend not to know you. But it is you who are pretending. You are pretending to have previously encountered me and discussed a jade when we did nothing of the kind. You have never been here before today. You have never seen myself nor Clint. I keep a register of everyone who visits this shop. You may look through it yourself and see if you are written there."

Schuler took the same binder out from the desk behind him and placed it delicately on the countertop. Then, he pawed through the greasy pages until he found the entry from two days ago.

"Here you are," he smiled with slimy satisfaction. "What did you say your name was?"

"I didn't say."

Each space in the page was occupied with a name and the time the person came scrawled out in the same handwriting that would make a doctor blush. The unsightly yellow smear was in the same spot, but "The Count of Monte Cristo", which I had so clearly seen Schuler write, was nowhere to be found.

Out of desperation disguised as curiosity, I looked for "Duryea", "Murdoch", and "Bigelow", but those names didn't appear. Not that they would. I started down at the sticky floor and pressed my teeth against each other.

"Do you see your name?" Schuler croaked.

I shook my head.

"I knew you would not. You must be a very sick man to imagine such things as this. How long have you suffered from these delusions? You must not allow them to continue. Seek mental health treatment before the condition worsens."

"He gave you the same script, huh?"

Schuler slowly shook his head. "Your case is a very serious one, indeed. It reminds me of my fifth cousin. The poor child was perfectly normal until he began having delusions that he had gone places he had never gone, and that he knew people he had never known. His parents ignored the condition, thinking it but a mere eccentricity as he came of age. And then he savagely attacked his classmate and would have slain him were it not for the intervention of those who witnessed the event.

His psychiatrist's diagnosis was so serious that he has been institutionalized since. It would be most unfortunate if such a thing happened to you."

"I'm fine," I said. "You and this runny nose got a payoff to make me think I'm a maniac, but it's not working. I know I'm as sound as the two of you put together, and I plan on staying that way."

The truth was, I was beginning to wonder myself. Whistling in the dark made more sense than doubting my own sanity, especially in front of those grunts, but all the way home I wondered about what I'd seen, or hadn't seen.

Duryea had approached me in Brody's, hadn't he? And Schuler had told me Nigel sold him the jade while Clint dripped snot all over the filthy floor, right? I wasn't delusional. I wasn't making up what I wanted to know, or what I thought I wanted to know, was I?

The stability of my soundness gnawed at me the rest of the afternoon, even as I listened to the third movement of Brahms' *Third Symphony*. I went to the piano, but the keys wouldn't cooperate.

I thought of Amthor, and Murdoch, and Duryea, and Schuler, all recommending my mental maladies be addressed. That was four different witnesses, however suspect, against my own sanity. And Amthor couldn't possibly have been on Murdoch's payroll, since he had come by before I even knew how Nigel was tied up in all of this. I scoffed at them until the possibility of their being right made it difficult for me to scoff.

No, I insisted. I wasn't insane. I wasn't imagining any of it. And yet, even if I was, my investigation wasn't going to be satisfied until it reached a resolution. By the end of the night, I intended to know whether Murdoch had the jade, or not.

17

THE LADY FROM SHANGHAI

By the time I weaved up Murdoch's winding driveway, it had started to sprinkle, but it didn't look like much would come of the clouds besides the typical, spitting spray that splatters cars with dust. Thunder cracked in the distance, and sounded like it would stay over there.

Yang was wearing a magua this time.

"Excuse please. You are?"

"A guy Murdoch wants locked away in the looney bin."

"Haw haw. Stranger who force into Mr. Murdoch house. Strange who underestimate surrounding."

"If you'd let me in, I wouldn't have to force into Mr. Murdoch house."

"Mr. Murdoch very busy man," Yang started to close the door.

I pushed the door open. "So am I."

The sickly aroma was just as nauseating as last time, but I didn't heave, and Yang didn't sneer.

"Where's the party?"

"Party?" Yang scoffed. "Mr. Murdoch not throw party."

"I didn't say he did. You make too many assumptions, Confucius."

"Who invite you party?"

"I did," said a voluptuous voice. Amelia appeared at the back of the foyer in a beautiful cheongsam with intricate azaleas detailed down to the dust on the petals. An unopened white umbrella was in her right hand. Some figure. Some face.

"You did well to come, Mr. Welles," she bit her bottom lip.

"Thanks for the invitation."

"It's refreshing to have any real man here, let alone one of your caliber."

"Your husband might not like that talk."

"Oh? And what might he do about it?"

"He might open that jar of bugs in his office and pour them on you while you sleep."

"But that sounds fun, and my husband is too austere to attempt anything that could be considered fun."

"Fun is a fetter on the sacred divinity of the soul."

Amelia giggled, took my arm, and leaned into me. Her perfume smelled like lotus combined with baby's breath.

We left the little man in the foyer and went down a narrow hall, past a marble carving of Shiva, across a maroon rug as long as a landing strip, and out an embellished door to the back yard.

An orange Oriental bridge with a roofed structure led over a pond with Balkhash Perches and northern snakeheads and Chinese sturgeons and Kyushu bitterlings and black stripe gudgeons and Ushimotsugo minnows. Various shrubs mixed with cherry blossom trees, circular bushes, stone pagodas that looked older than Genghis Khan, stone lions that looked like they weighed a ton each, and moss-covered rocks.

There was even an island in the center of the pond with a bonsai tree and two stone frogs with ruby eyes. I wondered if this place had been designated as a UNESCO World Heritage Site.

Several old Chinese men in Han fu dresses were playing flutes and harps to the tunes of traditional Eastern music. Murdoch listened approvingly, reclining near the pond in a changshan and an eboshi. He looked like a barefoot Merlin.

"Still looking into your friend?" Amelia asked, as we bypassed them and walked deliberately through the garden.

"Sure."

"Find any clues?"

"Some people might call them that."

"What might you call them?"

"Welts on my brain."

"I hope my husband didn't put them there."

"That would be too unenlightened for him. He would just hire somebody to do it."

"Certainly. Like all hypocrites, my husband seldom practices what he preaches. He may wax poetic about the great need for tolerance, but he hated Nigel. I don't know why my husband kept seeing him."

"Murdoch hated Nigel?"

"Very much. I never asked him why, but I didn't need to. I knew he was very jealous."

"Coquettes like you never appealed to Nigel."

"Well," Amelia blushed coyly. "You aren't very flattering to the hostess, are you? But I suppose you are right. Much as I made my feelings known to him, he didn't have any interest in me. He preferred that other girl."

"That other girl named Laura?"

"Nigel said so."

"How do you know Murdoch hated him? You didn't sit in on those boring appointments, did you?"

"No, but I know my husband, even if I don't particularly like him. After every time Nigel came, he mentioned Nigel's presence was troubling his soul. That's his way of saying he doesn't like somebody."

"You should've been a translator."

"An interesting profession," Amelia mused. "Much like yours."

"Mine's a dangerous profession."

"How so?"

"Murdoch reported me for insanity."

"He what?"

"Good thing a couple of fists fell on my head the other night, or I might not have found out. If he reports me two more times, the D.A. can petition to put me with the nuts. Murdoch know the D.A.?"

"Yes, they're very close. He comes over for dinner every month."

"So it's a cinch. They may not even bother with the petition."

"I can understand my husband's hatred of Nigel, because he perceived him to be a threat against himself. But he hardly knows you."

"Don't tell him that. He knows everything about everyone, even if he doesn't know anything about them."

"He hasn't even mentioned you since you came."

"How about Duryea? He mentioned him?"

"Duryea?"

"Sure, Duryea. The shamus he hired."

"He hired a shamus?"

"This isn't much of an act."

"I'm not acting, and I don't know who Duryea is."

"Never seen a guy up here with sneering silver eyes, blonde hair slicked back over his head, a dimpled chin that would make Kirk Douglas blush, bigger teeth than an elephant? He told me Murdoch hired him."

"Maybe so, but I never saw him. I don't always hang around the living room when strangers arrive, you know."

Those almond eyes locked on mine with a look that didn't need any explaining. What with Laura said, and what I had seen, I had a hard time believing she was as accepting of Nigel's indifference toward her as she was putting on.

18

ON DANGEROUS GROUND

When we came out of the garden, Murdoch was rubbing his fingertips across his eyebrows and making prolonged "ohum" sounds again. He acknowledged my presence with another one of those gestures like he was conducting an invisible orchestra.

"I see you have returned to a sanctuary which may find quiet to your soul," said he. "Are you willing to submit yourself to the enlightening stimulus of the East?"

"I guess I'd better. You'll have your pal the D.A. put me away if I don't."

Murdoch pulled his lips back like a horse and moved the other hand upward, like he was reaching for something on an invisible upper shelf. He emitted another "ohum" sound.

"Please do not continue to justify such measures, Mr. Welles. Sit, and enjoy the serenity of Eastern art that will be soon before you."

"Is Duryea part of the performance?" I sneered.

"Duryea?" Murdoch pretended to be puzzled. "No, I don't believe so. All our performers are from China, which renders performance more authentic thereby."

"How about Schuler?"

"Schuler?"

"You know who I mean."

"I do? Please, Mr. Welles, you're beginning to ramble again. Continue in this course, and you will leave me with no choice but to report you once more. There is no purpose to be unpleasant. Pray do not prohibit the enlightenment's spread by necessitating action against your insanity."

"I don't have any insanity, and you know it."

"Morris," Murdoch called over his shoulder, like he was summoning a bird.

The burly messenger, wearing a montsuki, trundled toward me with a sadistic smirk. I backed up within a pace of the pond, and wondered if there were giant fish in it that ate men Murdoch didn't like.

"Morris, Mr. Welles is exhibiting judgmental and schizophrenic tendencies. Such bigoted intolerance threatens to disrupt the performance. Moreover, I will be forced to report him for insanity once more, if his behavior does not improve. Ensure he conducts himself accordingly."

Morris ushered me to the back door. "It isn't wise to trouble Mr. Murdoch, friend."

"I guess so. Otherwise, he might shrink my head and put me in one of those little jars, wouldn't he, friend?"

"I don't think I ought to tell you, friend. You wouldn't enjoy the performance if I did."

He lumbered back to his post, occasionally glancing at Murdoch, occasionally glancing at me.

After a few minutes, a group of lithe, svelte Chinese girls who wore Han fu dresses and didn't look much older than twenty filed out of the back door with deferential nods to me and anyone else who saw them. Then, the music resumed and they started their graceful movements, like swans gliding across a lake.

As pleasant as this scene was, I hadn't come up here to enjoy it; I'd come up here to poke around the rest of this nutty house while Murdoch and his goons were distracted.

I started with that strange office, which had filtered the dim daylight into a serpentine gloom that made everything seem disproportionate. A bolt of lightning streaked across the sky and flashed a menacing burst of light into the room. Then came a boom of thunder, and the first droplets of rain began to roll down the window panes.

I looked through the distorted glass at a dark curtain of sky, where lightning stalked across the landscape from the west like a flamingo crossing a crocodile-laden swamp. I shrugged. We don't get rain in Albuquerque.

With the daylight worthless beyond making out the outlines of things, I used my phone flashlight to aid my search. The jars of fish and beetles and bugs glimmered eerily in the light. Every eye watched me with suspicion and hatred.

Murdoch's desk didn't have anything besides the same weird things that populated this freaky place. I combed the bookshelves, looked behind the pictures on the walls, even tapped on the chair that looked like a Thai throne to see if it had secret compartments. If Murdoch had the jade, he wasn't keeping it in here.

Steady rain pounded against the glass as I ascended the stairs. The lightning became brighter and thunder louder. If it was going to keep raining, it was only a matter of time before Murdoch and co. came inside. I'd better get going.

I came to another office, which was oriented similarly to the one downstairs but didn't have any jars of fish and beetles and bugs. It didn't have a jade, either.

What it did have was a laptop on the desk. The laptop's e-mail browser was open and a message from "Mindful Masters Weekly" was hawking some powder products for 20% off the regular price. I wondered if that was where Murdoch got his beetles.

Most of the messages – boring exchanges between Murdoch and his patients – confirmed the guy was a con artist. One of his victims had forked over five grand just for Murdoch to perform an Oriental dance he promised would bring the patient prosperity and good fortune. Another one had shelled out fifteen thousand so Murdoch would sprinkle beetle powder on his head to get the guy a job promotion. The sacred divinity of the soul was a good racket.

The rainfall began to roar, pounding the window sills, beating against the walls. As flashes of lightning cast the room in frightful shadow, I noticed Bigelow had sent an e-mail this morning which read:

Where is the shipment? You told me it would come last week. I strongly dislike delays.

Seeing the message had been replied to, I navigated to Murdoch's sent items inbox and found the response:

Impatience and an unseemly desire for instant gratification are two of the Western world's most prominent vices. Predictably, you struggle to comprehend the numerous stumblingblocks which can delay the arrival of goods being transported from lands thousands of miles from your own. In olden times, such a shipment would require six months of sailing, required no perils at sea befell the vessel. Our modern methods enable inestimably singular cargo to travel from East to West in a matter of days, yet you scorn this miraculous progress to exude ingratitude and entitlement.

Alas, I shall address the subject of your complaint. Yang has informed me the shipment was delayed due inventory malfunctions at the port of Shanghai. Now that the issue has been resolved, you shall receive the goods either this evening or tomorrow morning.

Hundreds of other e-mails like this went back many years. Murdoch wasn't just a weirdo; he was one of Bigelow's middlemen. He was a con artist and a racketeer.

I tried to connect Nigel to it all, but figured that would wait until I finished searching the rest of the house for the jade.

Still, I couldn't help but wonder if the jade was more than just a smuggled good. Maybe it was connected with something greater, something that would have turned Murdoch's criminal world upside down if the word got out. Maybe it was a personal, valuable keepsake that Murdoch wanted for himself. Or maybe it wasn't so, and that Nigel simply knowing what a fraud Murdoch is was enough to get him bumped off.

I slowly peeked into the corridor, where music and talking drifted up the stairs. As I expected, the performance had been moved indoors. I shut the door quietly and tiptoed down the hall to the next one. While I turned the knob, a bolt of lightning so loud I could hear its screeching struck and every light in the house went out.

I slipped into the next room and leaned against the door. More lightning flashed long enough for me to discern this was a bedroom. Two large, east-facing windows, as well as a glass balcony door, were open and the furious rainfall was splashing in off the sills and the tiles.

From the aroma of lotus and baby's breath, I'd say this was Amelia's bedroom. A plush, traditional Chinese bed sat opposite an antique Chinese dresser. There was a chaise lounge and another Chinese chair flanking the bed, and an Oriental room divider with a peacock painted on its surface stood in the northeast corner.

Too much noise was coming from the rain for me to know should somebody walk down the hallway, so I closed everything without caring if Murdoch suspected I did it, or not. As I was reaching into my pocket for my phone, however, I felt the sensation I was being watched. I flipped on the flashlight just in time to catch a blow to the back of my head.

The lightning and the thunder and the downpour and the house's freakish atmosphere all faded away as a deep, dark pool opened up before me. I plunged in.

19

NIGHTMARE ALLEY

Vague remembrances. Distorted sounds. Twisted memories. Strange dreams.

All I had come across since my investigation started – Patty's hideous visage, Brody's smirking busboy, Duryea's sneering smile, Laura's fair loveliness, Murdoch's reserved malice – blended together against a backdrop of those rambunctious tunes I had heard Fitch's troupe play. But it had a quality like everything was underwater.

Giant trumpets flared up before me. Clarinets were stretched like they were rubber. Drums as big as water tanks were pummeled. Pianos were pounded like somebody was taking the keys in his hands and squeezing them until they shrieked.

Too loud. It was all much too loud. Compared to this ruckus, that dingy little room downtown was as quiet as a country churchyard.

Away went the jazz. Now, I was suspended by a narrow string above Murdoch's pond, which was filled with crocodiles and pythons instead of obscure fish. The string lowered me closer and closer while its threads peeled off, one by one.

Then I wasn't dangling anymore. I was in a room with no windows and no doors and no ceiling, watched by a thousand enormous eyes that blinked angrily at my every move. Voices exhibited pleasure over my plight, voices that shrieked and snarled and sneered and roared and raged with a beastly cadence that made my body clammy with agitated sweat.

The eyes disappeared, and the Far East took its place. The musicians from Murdoch's garden were there, cranking out swing jazz with flutes and harps that sounded like trumpets and clarinets.

Besides the musicians, all those images and statues and tapestries and jars I had seen in Murdoch's house were alive and debating what the best means of disposing of me were. I was prompted to open an ornately embellished drawer and found a sword glittering in the top shelf. I seized it and smashed jars and impaled chairs and dismembered statues that lunged at me with spears. Then everything was dark again.

Before I could see, or hear, or taste, or smell, I felt a sensation like electric currents running through my veins and pulsing at wavering intervals. Then, I felt wet and wondered if that pool I had plunged into was Murdoch's pond.

A light gradually came into view, an orange light filtered through a distorted prism. My focus improved enough to perceive a lantern hung from the ceiling. That, and a tapestry of cranes at a lake, was enough to tell me where I was.

The rest of my senses were gradually recalibrating. My skin was clammy and my throat felt like it had been coated with sand. The thought of lifting my head was a struggle, so I tried to move my limbs instead, only to discover I was fastened to a long bench with gilt upholstery.

Sweat trickled down my cheeks. I wondered what time it was. I wondered what day it was. I could have been out five hours or five days. Maybe twenty years had gone by, and I had grown a long, gray beard like Rip Van Winkle.

A door crawled open. A head like a lightbulb poked into the room, and two yellow eyes watched me while luminous lips formed a satisfied smirk.

Murdoch took swift, silent strides and sat in another Chinese chair at my elbow. Morris followed him into the room and shut the door like it was a thousand years old and made of fine China and would disintegrate if you breathed near it. He stood menacingly behind Murdoch, his eyes flickering with pleasure at my predicament.

"What was your first thought upon awakening, Mr. Welles?" Murdoch inquired placidly.

"I wished I had Genghis Khan's sword to cut you in half," I grumbled. My tongue felt like it had been removed, salted, hung out in the sun for a week, and then sewed back into my throat with wool.

"This proves what I have suspected from the beginning: violence is the consuming passion of your heart. Only disturbed minds meditate upon violence so thoroughly they desire to manifest it even after their senses have been temporarily disabled. Your insanity is evident, whether you wish to acknowledge it, or not."

"Haven't you heard of sarcasm?"

"Do not attempt to disguise your depravity with the veil of sarcasm. Cases as yours have only one solution."

"Your slimeball pal the D.A. still has to petition for me to be put away."

Murdoch rubbed his eyebrows with his fingertips and sighed. "You are mistaken once more, Mr. Welles. Those conditions are not necessary, if the person in question demonstrates violent and insane behavior, and you have already done so. Therefore, the conditions *have* been satisfied. But, even if you had not done so, my 'slimeball pal', as you call him, would have happily accelerated the process to ensure you will be put where all troubled souls belong. I am recording this conversation, just as I have recorded our previous ones, and will edit them accordingly in the event they are needed."

"Violent and insane behavior? You mean like smacking a guy and pumping dope into him?"

"'Dope' is a rather crass designation for medicine of such sophistication. But I shall not delay what is necessary any further. My first reporting you for insanity was intended to be a warning to discourage you from continuing this investigation. Unfortunately, you did not heed. The sacred divinity of the soul could have done you much mindful good, if only you had not rejected it with bigoted hatred."

"What did you do with my car? And my phone?"

"Morris took the liberty of returning your phone and car to your residence. It seemed the appropriate action to take, considering they will be of no further use to you."

"That's what you think."

"It is not merely what I *think*, Mr. Welles; it is what I *know*. I likewise know you entered my sanctum and accessed my personal laptop. I gave you the serum merely to discover the extent of your findings. No malice motivated the deed."

"That makes me feel a lot better about everything."

Murdoch let out another one of those stupid "ohum" sounds. I was getting to hate those. I was getting to hate everything about him and his sordid schemes and his freakish abode.

“Your contempt and scorn for the East, and my interpretations of it, manifest in your every word – nay, in your every expression. There is no benefit to explaining things you will only despise.”

“Why did you pay off Duryea and Schuler?”

“Duryea? Schuler? How should I know who they are?”

“Don’t play dumb. You paid them to pretend they’d never seen me before.”

“Please, Mr. Welles, do not persist in these maniacal ramblings. You do yourself no benefit by demonstrating the depths of your insanity.”

“I’m not insane, and you know it.”

“I wish I did know that. It would save us all a great deal of trouble, if it were true. Alas, we cannot simply wish things into reality. The matter is, you are deeply disturbed. If you had kept your insanity to yourself, perhaps such drastic measures would not be necessary. But when you manifest violence and threaten to perpetuate it, action is required. Your soul must be replenished before it inflicts harm upon others. I wish you radiant contentment, Mr. Welles.”

As soon as Murdoch had left, Morris deliberately approached. A depraved smile flashed across his face as he took a small case out of his pocket and opened it like a child unwrapping a Christmas present.

Inside was a needle filled with a gray, gelatinous liquid, like some primordial slime that had been extracted from a pyterodactyl's brain. I tried to free myself, but I felt like I was tied down by iron chains.

"Do not struggle, friend," Morris sneered. "Struggling does not profit you. It only makes the inevitable more unpleasant."

I pushed to no avail. It was all I could do to lift my head.

"Where do you want it, friend? I suggest the right arm, along the tricep. How does that sound, friend?"

I kept squirming, like a worm about to be devoured by a robin. Morris snickered as he plunged the needle into my arm. There was no deep, dark pool this time. Just a bolt of pain and curtains of darkness.

20

CRACK UP

Somebody was screaming. At first, it sounded like it was a block away. Then, it started to get louder, and louder, until it was practically next to my ear.

My eyes fluttered open and caught glimpses of a circular light that shone coldly on me. I shut my eyes until they could tolerate the brightness and tried to put my finger on the sound. Amidst the screaming were murmuring voices.

"Better call Frank," one of them muttered.

"Frank hates his guts," said the other.

"So what? Call Frank."

In a bed about two feet to the left was a bald guy with sunburned skin, staring up at the ceiling and pounding his fists into a pillow while emitting bloodcurdling shrieks.

I was in a bed myself, a deformed, sagging bed with a thin sheet and a rusted metal frame and iron straps at both ends. The whole ward was full of beds full of guys making strange noises, and rustling with the pillows, and clawing at the frame, and talking to people that weren't there.

One was emitting deranged cackles. Another was shouting like he was watching a horse race. Another was debating the superiority of mechanical pencils to traditional ones. Another was moving his arms upward like he was climbing an invisible ladder.

More cold lights ran along a concrete ceiling upheld by four concrete walls that didn't have anything on them but a clock and a few windows with iron bars you could hardly see through. The clock said it was just before two; given how dark it looked outside, I didn't think it was afternoon.

Still, the place was spacious, for a nuthouse. I could stretch my arms out both ways, and I would only hit the other guy's shoulder.

The two voices I had heard belonged to well-built men in their early thirties, wearing white scrubs, watching the spectacle with scowls and folded arms.

"When's he gonna shut up?" snarled the taller of the two.

"Frank'll make him shut up. That's why you were supposed to call him."

"I *did* call him."

"Then why isn't he here?"

"He was busy. Some creep tried to cut off his arm."

"Nolan again?"

"No, Lloyd."

"Lloyd?"

"Yeah, Lloyd. Don't act so surprised. He tried to bite you last week."

"A lot of them tried to bite me last week."

A phone buzzed. The taller of the two scrubs pulled one out and stuffed it back into his pocket.

"Frank's on his way," he grumbled.

"Isn't that courteous of him?"

A few minutes later, a metal door in the right corner of the opposite wall swung open, and Frank stomped in. He wore a doctor's coat, but he didn't have a stethoscope, and he carried his clipboard without scowling at it like the E.R. doctor.

"Reynolds again," the taller one told him.

"Did you give him the pills?" Frank asked with a deep, cold voice, like water at the bottom of an iceberg.

"Who, me?" the taller one shrugged.

"Did you give him the pills?" Frank asked the shorter one.

"Who, me?" the shorter one smirked.

"How many times do I have to tell you to give him the pills?" Frank snapped as he took a pen out of his coat and scribbled something angrily onto the clipboard. At least he wasn't scowling at it.

"Try giving him the pills yourself," the taller one snickered. "See if he doesn't try to tear your arms off first."

"If you gave him the pills when you should, he wouldn't *try* to tear your arms off first," Frank huffed.

"Sure, he would," the shorter one snapped. "Why do you think he's in this freak stable in the first place?"

Frank shook his head and looked back at the clipboard.

"We'd better get him into isolation," he said while thoughtfully nibbling on the cap of the pen. "Get Grant and Hugo in here with a straight-jacket."

"Just one?" the taller one snickered.

"Just one," Frank snarled. He stomped over to the door and scanned a card on the wall and stomped out once it opened.

"Where's Grant and Hugo?" the taller one asked.

"Downstairs. They're gonna stay down there when they find out why we want them up here."

"Then say it's their great uncle from Dublin wanting to tell them a bedtime story."

"You tell them. I'm not gonna stay up here listening to this nut."

The shorter one walked to the door, scanned a card, waited for the door to open, and went out just like Frank had.

The taller one pulled out the phone and dialed a number. When nobody answered, he shrugged, stuffed it into his pocket, walked to the door, scanned a card, waited for the door to open, and went out just like Frank and the shorter one had.

I sat up. My skin looked weird under these lights. Everything looked weird under these lights. I wasn't sweating any more, but my skin was still clammy, and my senses were still off, and Murdoch's drugs were still in my system. Staying in this nuthouse wasn't going to help my convalescence.

Even if I had managed to open a window, a gnat couldn't have fit between those bars. The only way out was the door, and the only way to open it was one of those handy cards that Frank and the two grumbling nurses had. I considered ambushing them when they returned and darting out then and there, but this wouldn't work because I knew nothing about this place's layout and wasn't likely to figure it out in a frantic state of mind.

The door swung open again, and a guy that looked like a psycho Ken doll slithered into the room. As he scoured the beds, his proud green eyes twinkled with lunacy and deviant smugness spread across his face. Then, he saw my bed, and unfurled a white hospital gown like it was a banner.

"I'm Biff," he purred.

"Glad to hear it."

"It's good to be glad, Welles. Especially when you're in the middle of a crack up. Put on your gown."

"Why don't you wear it? It fits you better."

"There's a thought. But I'd rather see you put it on. It'd give me a lot of pleasure."

He rolled the gown into a ball and hurled it at me. I ducked. The gown hit the wall and slid behind the bed.

"And I just had it washed and ironed," Biff leered while lurching along the bed. "Just had it washed and ironed, only for you to make it dirty. You know, there's a lot of nasty things behind this bed, Welles. A lot of creepy things. A lot of slimy things. A lot of disgusting things. Do you want to look back there, Welles? Do you want to see what I'm describing?"

Biff pulled the gown out and dangled it a few inches from my face. It was caked with dust and dark stains.

"Go on, Welles. Wear it. Make Biff glad. Make Biff real glad."

He shoved the gown at me, so I rolled to the side, ripped it out of his hands, and flung it to the door.

"An impressive throw. But you shouldn't have done that, Welles. It made me upset. You don't want to see me upset."

"Get lost, creep."

"Biff, a creep? That's not very nice language, Welles. You should talk sweetly to me, because I can do a lot of things *for* you, or I can do a lot of things *to* you. I can do *anything* I want to you, and *nobody's* going to stop me. You know why, Welles? Because you're a lunatic.

"I'm no lunatic."

"Oh yes, you are. You're insane, Welles, whether you think you are, or not. That's why they brought you here. So you could fellowship with your own kind. So you could share a room with twenty other maniacs just like you. Sure, some of them spill their blood all over the floor because they think they've got cockroaches crawling under their skin. Some of them try to jump out windows and break through ceilings because they see the devils are after them. Some of them bend bed frames and bite through chains like they're nothing more than pasta noodles. But, deep down, you're all the same. You all belong together. A kinship of nuts. A community of freaks.

A commune of the depraved and delirious and demented and degenerate and disturbed."

"Give me your card, scum."

"What a laugh. The new nut hasn't been here an hour, and he's already figuring on getting out. You must have missed the memo, Welles. Once you get in here, you're never getting out. Oh, sure, you can try. You can try to run out, or walk out, or jump out, or climb out, or crawl out, or claw out, but they'll get you every time. You won't escape. You can't escape."

Biff stopped snickering, tackled me onto the ground and tried to put me in a chokehold.

"Stop struggling, Welles. Let me have my way, and I'll forget all about this. I won't even tell the administrators. Krauss didn't let me have my way, and I told them to put him in isolation. You won't like isolation, Welles. You aren't really by yourself. You're in with the rats, and the cockroaches, and the spiders, and big beetles that bite and fly. I don't bite nearly as hard as they do, Welles."

I kicked him off me before he could demonstrate. He wiped the blood off his mouth slowly, bared his teeth like a carnivore about to catch its prey, and whipped a knife out from his scrubs.

"Don't think I won't do it, Welles. I've carved up plenty of nuts with this blade."

The guy that had been screaming leaped onto Biff with fury. Amidst the carnage, I snatched his card, scanned it, and crept into the hall.

A nurse looking at his phone leaned against a wall ten feet down, but he didn't notice me. I tiptoed around the opposite corner to an elevator and a door leading to a flight of stairs. I scanned the card again and tore down them noiselessly.

At the bottom of the stairs, another door with a scanner waited. Behind it was another nurse about to go up the elevator.

"Where's your uniform?" he frowned.

"My uniform? How can I have a uniform when I just started working here?"

"They didn't give you a uniform?"

"No, they didn't. Is that my fault?"

"All right, Mac, keep your shirt on."

He went into the elevator; I sighed in relief and went through the sliding doors and out into the night.

21

ACE IN THE HOLE

There wasn't time to appreciate the refreshing outside air, because a truck traversing the parking lot was about to blast me with its beams. I crouched behind cacti until it passed and looked with fearful wonder at the building from which I had fled.

Five stories of mauve brick and terror, built early last century in the diagonal pattern popular for nuthouses then, loomed against the sky. Ivy crawled across stone balconies that jutted out maniacally and sinister turrets that towered menacingly. But it was the things inside – the things that sneered and slithered and screamed – that made my hair stand on end.

This parking lot was bounded by thick brick walls twenty feet high and topped with intertwined electrical and barbed wires. Two hundred feet down, the wall gave way to an iron gate where a guard was stationed in a small booth. Showing him Biff's card and saying I was walking home wasn't going to fly.

The truck had stopped in front of the sliding doors, where a guy in his late twenties had gotten out of the driver's side and shuffled into the dreadful place. By the time he came out, I had hoisted myself into the bed.

He turned the ignition none the wiser and whipped through the lot. A brief stop at the gate while it opened, and we were off. I didn't feel sentimental about leaving.

After a couple of minutes, the road flattened from its decline. He turned left and began to haul it, past fifty miles per hour, then sixty, seventy, eighty. Clinging to the sides of the bed, I felt like Coleridge's ancient mariner while the spirits sped the ship across the sea. Shapes whirled by me too quickly to perceive.

When I came to, the truck was stopped. I didn't think this guy was the kind that stopped at red lights. I didn't think this guy was the kind that stopped, period. I guess I was wrong. I guess I was wrong about a lot of things – who bumped off Nigel, and why, being chief among them.

We were at the intersection of Lomas and San Pedro. Matt Duryea's office was in the neighborhood, but he was only an ancillary piece to a puzzle I was starting to put together. When all this was settled, maybe I'd drop by again. We could talk over old times while he smirked and I walloped him into the wall.

I stayed in the bed for another few blocks until it became clear the guy wasn't going where I wanted to go. I hopped out and walked to Laura's. Only a boor would bang on the door at this ungodly hour, so I plopped on the porch and tossed all that had passed up to this point around my mind until day.

"Preston?" Laura asked with astonishment. A white bathrobe was draped along her figure, but it wasn't half as pale as her face.

"Surprised much?"

"What, what's the matter?"

"I'm in a jam. Care to hear an explanation?"

She nodded and we went into the breakfast nook and watched birds lay waste to a colony of worms. I explained all that had happened since I'd sneaked up to Bigelow's office. Laura listened intently and silently, save for an occasional gasp.

"I called you last night, Preston. I was worried since you said you were going back to Murdoch's. If something happened to you..." Quiet weeping succeeded her words.

"Laura," I said gently.

"I should have told you before," she resumed after a few seconds. "I wanted to tell you that night at The Parthenon. That's why I called. When you didn't answer, I was afraid I had missed my chance to tell you. I was afraid something had happened to you, like Nigel."

"You can tell me now."

"Darling, I want to be with you from now on. I don't want to ever be apart from you anymore. You see, I love you."

Something about her was suspicious. Maybe it was my getting knocked around after I'd dropped her off that night. Maybe it was her transferring her affection from Nigel to me in a matter of days. Maybe it was her looking like she'd seen a ghost when she answered the door.

But the hazel eyes. The gentle cheeks. The luscious lips. No guy in his right mind would walk away from all of that on account of circumstantial evidence. After all, she was the kind that poets had scrawled their finest verses in praise of, that painters had limned with their loveliest strokes, that musicians had captivated with their most beauteous rhythms.

"I'm crazy about you too."

"Do you mean it, Preston?"

"I mean it."

She emitted a squeal of joy and kissed me. My doubts were on life support. Still, I had just broken out of the nuthouse and needed to come up with a plan. She agreed I should stay here, at least until I came up with a better idea, because the first place the law would look would be my house. In the meanwhile, she prepared me a bounty of food.

"Preston," she said after I'd wolfed down everything in sight. "I have a key to Murdoch's house."

"Huh?"

"Nigel gave it to me for safekeeping. He didn't want somebody else to get it if something happened to him."

"How'd he get Murdoch's key?"

"He never told me. Maybe he had a copy made, or maybe he swiped it off him, or maybe *she* gave him one. I mention this, because I overheard Whit last night say Murdoch and that woman would be out of town for several days. You could get his laptop and show the police what you saw. It might even have those recordings he made of you."

"He goes out of town and just leaves his laptop lying around?" I snorted. "That doesn't make sense. If he didn't take it with him, he would put it somewhere secure."

"Nigel told me Murdoch has another laptop that he takes whenever he goes somewhere. It's a superstition of his. He thinks leaving the same laptop in the same place will bring him good fortune."

"Even if I get the laptop, the law will still want to put me back in that looney bin. They're not going to listen to me."

"But they'll listen to me. My father is good friends with the chief. He would listen. I know he would."

"Haven't you heard? In this rotten society, a man is guilty until proven innocent. Even if they would listen to you, they wouldn't just let me off the hook. They'd want a hearing and have me prove my case. They might even have me go back there first."

"No, they wouldn't," she said earnestly. "I would make them promise me they wouldn't."

"Their promises aren't worth much."

"Wouldn't it be worth much to have yourself declared sane and free? Your only alternative is hiding out, Preston. That's no way to live."

"Maybe I can think of something better," I muttered. "Something that clears my name without having to depend on a crooked court system."

"Please, Preston, listen to me. I know this will work out. Won't you do it? Won't you trust me?"

Sure, I couldn't hide forever, but at least that would buy me time, time for my mind to clear and for Murdoch's dope to get out of my system and for me to devise a solution more surefire than this. I looked at her again, but that was a mistake. One glance at that heavenly face was all it took to turn my "no" into a "yes."

"Fine."

"It's the right thing choice, darling," Laura assured me sweetly. "We'll all be glad that you did, in the end."

"Think so?"

"Oh, yes, I know it will be the best thing for all of us. It may not seem like it now, but it will. I'll pick you up after rehearsals and drive you to Murdoch's house. Since you know where the laptop is, it shouldn't take more than five minutes to get it. Then, we'll come back here and go to the police with the laptop tomorrow."

There was a part of me that didn't like this idea at all. Too many things could go wrong. Murdoch could come back unexpectedly. Morris and Yang could be lurking. The law could be watching the place and ambush me the minute I got out of the car. And even if I did get the laptop unscathed, there was no guarantee the cops would listen to Laura, even if her old man was chums with the chief.

No, I didn't like it at all. I didn't like the atmosphere of the glowering clouds that reflected dispirited gray light through the window. I didn't like the solitary sensation what I had just agreed to produced. My mind was tied in a Gordian knot.

I was about to phone Laura to call the whole thing off when her charm – the same charm Nigel had referenced – made me think otherwise. Bewitching, that charm. I saw no reason to go through with this, but I was going through with it anyway.

Sure, she and her plan seemed suspicious. But the dame was crazy about me, crazy enough to stick her neck out and concoct this wild scheme just for the slight chance of clearing my name. If it went sideways, she'd be an accessory to unlawful entering and directly responsible for aiding a lunatic. But she proposed it anyway, even though she had little to gain and plenty to lose by it.

If a girl with gumption like Laura was so certain this would work, a girl with a mind that hadn't been slapped silly several times and pumped full of drugs, maybe I should be, too. Maybe my uneasiness over going back to Murdoch's was getting the better of me, clouding my foresight, distorting my judgement.

After all, I was a grown man. I knew what tricks Murdoch had up his sleeves. And, like Laura said, making an attempt like this was infinitely better than holing up from place to place without a plan. As Carlyle wrote, all doubt can only be ended by action. I watched the day go by and waited for the night to come.

22

CRISS CROSS

A sultry day had given way to a sultry night. Murky moonlight filtered through the hazy sky like a flashlight through a translucent window. The heavy gray clouds that had dominated the afternoon soon swept it all away.

There wasn't much conversation as we rode to Murdoch's house, besides rehashing what we had earlier discussed. She was to park two houses before his as a precaution, and I was to signal her with my flashlight if somebody was inside.

The houses on Murdoch's dark street loomed silent and suspicious. I was beginning to lose my optimism again when Laura parked and put a gentle hand on mine. Something about being around her gave me hope I wouldn't have ordinarily had.

"Don't worry about it, darling," she smiled reassuringly. "Within five minutes, you'll be back in this car as if nothing suspenseful had happened. You'll see."

I held the key in my hand and looked at Murdoch's gate. Then, I turned back to her.

"And you'll be waiting here when I get out."

"Of course I will, dearest," she replied as she leaned forward. "You can depend on me."

Then, she kissed me strongly and clutched me harder than I was clutching Murdoch's house key.

"Good luck, Preston," she whispered as she gently removed her lips from mine.

Murdoch's plants were somber and subdued in the darkness. I thought about turning on my flashlight, but somebody might see it, and the last thing I needed now was attention. I felt for the lock and let the key work its magic.

A dark chasm of black opened up before me, like the pool I'd dove into on that rainy night in this eerie place. I entered without fear, but didn't lock the door, in case I needed to make a quick exit. The sickly aroma was as nauseating as ever, but I couldn't let that bother me now.

It was quiet enough in here to hear a man blink. A lantern that hung aloft of the stairs threw that familiar, distorted light onto the banister. I took each step swiftly and came to the upstairs office door. After a deep breath, I went in.

The laptop was shut and begging for me to take it out of this wacky house to somewhere sane, somewhere without bugs in jars and prisms of nutty light and an atmosphere that weighed more than an elephant. I was walking across the rug with the laptop in hand when the door swung open and a familiar shape strode into the room.

"Are you leaving so soon, Mr. Welles?" Murdoch asked placidly, like he had been expecting my company and was displeased at the thought of losing it so quickly.

"What are you doing here?"

"Here? This happens to be my house, Mr. Welles," he smiled imperturbably as he sat down at the desk and turned on the lamp. "I will not berate you for forgetting the fact. Insanity takes a ponderous toll on the mind."

Two rough guys I'd seen once before shut the door. One of them took the laptop from me at gunpoint and set it back on the desk like it had never left.

"Anyone for tennis?" I asked meagerly.

"Mr. Welles, Feet and Mitts. I trust you have had the pleasure of making their acquaintance."

"You're Eyebrows Da Silva," I muttered as much to myself as to Murdoch.

"Yes," Murdoch sighed as he lighted a hookah's coals. "You do not catch on very fast, do you, Mr. Welles? That is pitiable. If your mind had been nourished by the sacred divinity of the soul, you could have saved yourself much difficulty. Such folly as yours perfectly epitomizes the plight of Western man. He is offered a convincing warning of what peril awaits him, but he obstreperously ignores it to his own ruin. Ignorance and stubbornness are inseparable inmates of the same bosom."

"Why did you have these mugs bump off Nigel?" I asked. "Because Amelia wanted him? Or because he found out who you were and was going to rat you out?"

"There is little truth to what you say, Mr. Welles. Your friend Nigel knew very little about me – certainly not as much as you do. He also had very little to do with my wife, even though she would have preferred he had. That did not bother her, for rejection only amuses Amelia. She is verily a singular specimen, and quite materialistic for one bred in the Orient, but that is acceptable to me. I have never attempted to exhibit love which doubtless would not be requited. The only lover which ever could attract my affection is who I have labored on behalf of in disposing of you. She commanded these henchmen to administer violence to you, and killed Nigel."

"You sent them after me," I said, though I didn't think now he had. "You were afraid I'd find out what Nigel found out about you."

Murdoch slowly shook his head and weaved another strange gesture with his hands, like he was back to conducting that invisible orchestra. I hoped this would be the final symphony.

"You are too credulous a creature, for all the judgement and bigoted suspicion you exude. Nigel only visited me because he thought I had a jade which Whit Bigelow coveted. Foolish of Nigel, to think so. Foolish of Whit, to be so ignorant of my collection after our many years of smuggling. Do you know who told Whit I had this jade, Mr. Welles? The same which engineered Nigel's demise and has been manipulating you from the beginning. Poor Western man. He prides himself in logic and sound reasoning, yet the mere sight of a beautiful woman disarms his reason."

Murdoch puffed from the hookah. I glanced hurriedly around the room for a means of escape. There weren't any, unless I clicked my heels together and said, "There's no place like home."

"I concede I played a part in your being committed to the asylum," Murdoch smiled with satisfaction. "And in arranging for unsavory persons to make you doubt your sanity. Verily, it was our objective to drive you out of your mind, whereby you would be institutionalized without any recommendation on my behalf. We had greater plans in place which would have made your insanity evident to all, but your decision to trespass in my private office expedited matters. I may be a racketeer, but I also happen to be a psychiatrist who isn't deeply disturbed, rare as that may be, and I do not think it is scrupulous to take credit for plans that another contrived."

"An honorable quack," I snorted.

"To drive you insane was never my idea," he shrugged. "I was simply following orders. My real love thought your investigation could be troublesome, and she asked me to help dispose of you. Since she promised to marry me as my reward, I complied with zeal. I do not think it is scrupulous to take credit for plans that another contrived. I may be a racketeer, but I also happen to be a psychiatrist who isn't deeply disturbed, rare as that may be. But I shall not further delay the inevitable. Feet and Mitts will personally escort your return to the asylum. Pray do not resist their instructions, Mr. Welles. You are a wanted man, and any act of violence can be justified against a raving lunatic. She told me so herself; truthfully, the idea gave her much pleasure."

"You're bluffing."

"For your sake, I wish I were. Howbeit, to perish..."

Guns were fired. Murdoch's smirk disappeared as he slumped forward in his chair. I ripped open the door and narrowly avoided a wall of bullets as I flung myself into the hallway.

"Don't run away, Tolstoy," Mitts' sneer followed me down the stairs, but the two brutes stayed behind to reload. The problem was Morris lurked at the bottom of the stairs and wielded a sword like the one in my nightmare. Yang, holding a blow dart, stood a pace behind him.

"Going somewhere, friend?" Morris snickered. His eyes flamed with sadism.

"Haw haw," Yang sneered. "Stranger that force into Mr. Murdoch house have difficult experience."

I flipped myself over the side of the banister just before the bullets went back to whizzing. As Morris and Yang were felled, I scrambled to the door and yanked it open and bolted out into the night, past the stone lions and the laughing Buddhas and the bamboo and the asters and the jasmine for what surely would be the last time. With somebody firing at me from an upstairs window, the laptop was the farthest thing from my mind.

“Start it, Laura!” I shouted as I scaled the gate.

The car was gone.

“Laura?” I called out in despair. My brain swirled in dismay. My soul squirmed in despair.

The car was gone. She was gone with it.

23

FAREWELL, MY LOVELY

I didn't have time to reflect on the ramifications of this, because Feet and Mitts were over the gate and back to firing away. One bullet scraped the sidewalk near my shoes; another sailed past my ear.

"Come back here, chum," Mitts crooned nastily. "We gots a little surprise for you. We want to take you on a little trip."

"Yeah, Tolstoy," Feet seconded. "We'd like to take you for a little ride."

I had no car, no laptop, and no plan. The only solution was to outrun their fists and feet and bullets. I made for the theater.

Everything was engulfed by the sheer blackness of the night. Lanes with no street lights were draped in darkness, the houses that lined them absorbed in the menacing wall of midnight.

Here and there, a solitary, weak street lamp would throw some pitiful light into the black, like a candle wafting in a lightless crypt. Beyond the threshold of the darkness, it felt like a thousand eyes were watching me.

The night became bleaker, darker, gloomier. Darkness surged from alleys, seeped over rooftops, oozed out of windows. And the sneering corruption and contemptible cruelty of the city was present in every sidewalk crack, in every dilapidated edifice, in every strip of peeling paint, in every chunk of crumbling stucco.

More and more people appeared as I walked up Central, enough so that Feet and Mitts had to tuck their toys away and walk like respectable gentleman out for an evening stroll. The problem was, the closer we got to the theater, the fewer people we came across, until the streets were practically empty at Central and University Boulevard.

“Don’t be going along all by yourself, Tolstoy,” Mitts tauntingly admonished as he pulled his gun out and restocked it. “It isn’t safe to walk alone down an empty street at night.”

“You heard him, mug,” Feet said. “Why don’t you come with us? We’ll look out for you. We’ll keep you safe.”

I darted behind the street light in time to dodge two bullets. Then, I was off and running again.

The fastest route to the theater was sure to fill me with lead, so I cooked up a circuitous route by darting south on University and behind a series of parked cars. Bullets shattered the glass and punctured the doors as I crawled east into a trash-filled alley between two decaying buildings.

"C'me here, mug," Feet shouted.

"Did you notice that, Feet?" Mitts snickered from the mouth of the alley. "Tolstoy don't feel so talkative today."

"He's wasting a chance to use his words," Feet observed. "They don't let him use his words where he's going."

"And he don't have need for no words, where he's going," Mitts added.

Their invisible couriers of death kept following me, clanging off dumpsters and screeching off brick walls and screaming into the dark abyss at the back. I leapt over a chain link fence at the east end of the alley, only to walk straight into a haymaker.

"That's better," Mitts sneered while Feet added a kick. "Now, we're making progress. It's good for a guy to get exercise, Tolstoy. Especially a guy that's going where you're going."

"I'm not going back there," I spat as I climbed to my feet.

"Did you hear that, Feet? Tolstoy says he's not going back there."

"Presumptuous punk, ain't he?" Feet smirked.

“Real presumptuous,” Mitts concurred as he unsheathed the gun again. “But we gots a way of fixing that.”

He smacked me with the stock of the gun, then with the back of his empty hand. Feet tried to trample me, but when I rolled out of the way, he settled for another sharp kick to the stomach instead.

“You see, chum?” Mitts grinned. “You should’ve listened to us. We didn’t want to have to knock you around, but you ain't left us with no choice.”

“You rats are gonna get the chair,” I coughed as I struggled to stand. “You’re gonna get the chair for what you did to Nigel. I hope they let me throw the switch.”

“Did you hear that, Feet? Tolstoy says we’re gonna get the chair, and that he’s gonna throw the switch.”

“Kinda screwy to give guys the chair for things they didn’t do,” Feet remarked.

“Kinda hard to throw the switch from the nuthouse."

“Don’t think about beating it, Tolstoy,” Feet advised me after I’d managed to stand up. “We’re only supposed to hold our fire if you come with us.”

“Sure, Tolstoy,” Mitts said. “Nobody’d object to a couple of respectable guys gunning down a deranged maniac that broke out of the looney bin. We'd get medals pinned on us down at the city hall."

"So don't try it," Feet snarled. "It's in your best interest. Besides, you got out of that place before. Maybe you can get out of it again. And this time, maybe you'll be smart enough not to let yourself get talked into something that don't make sense."

People appeared on a nearby sidewalk along Buena Vista Drive. The two brutes wouldn't dare firing into a crowd, so I pushed Mitts into Feet and took off. By the time they had recovered, I was across the street and nearing the theater.

Back to the present. Back to Beethoven. Back to the world and the flesh and the devil and Laura. Back to where it all began, in this place, between these walls, under this roof, above this stage.

Like I said, fitting. Ironic.

The symphony was nearing its finish now. I staggered out of my seat and went backstage, just like I had the first time. Only Ridgley wasn't dragging my elbow, and I wasn't going to politely withdraw if Laura didn't answer the door.

Here was the hall. It was quiet today. No stage workers scurrying around like ants. No swan maidens to carry out conversation with. Just dark and silent and sullen. I knocked on her dressing door resolutely and waited.

"Come to see your sweetheart, Mr. Welles?" sneered a voice out of the darkness, a voice like the sound of biting into a fresh apple.

Bigelow emerged from the back of the hall, holding a revolver in his right hand.

"I underestimated the resilience of your chivalry," he smiled nastily. "Be sensible and don't waste any more of it on her. Doing so would be akin to casting your pearls before swine."

"What'd you do to her?"

"What did I do to her?" Bigelow frowned. "That's an interesting question. Why should I do anything to her, Mr. Welles? I've wanted Laura for a very long time. Surely, she told you I was jealous of your friend Wilfred. That would seem to contradict the possibility of my inflicting harm upon her, wouldn't you say, Mr. Welles?"

"That gun doesn't think so."

"The gun? That's right, there was something in the news about your being put away. What else does the gun think? Please tell me. I'm fascinated by your clairvoyance."

"What are you doing here?"

"I've a few things to straighten out with Laura. You might have heard your friend Wilfred was supposed to steal a jade for me, but I haven't gotten it yet."

"Then who has it?"

"You aren't particularly fast witted, Mr. Welles. Wilfred did not have the jade. I do not have the jade. That leaves Murdoch and Laura."

"What about Amelia?"

"To suppose she would have anything to do with it is absurd."

Just then, Laura opened her door and came into the hallway, wearing Odette's costume as she had on that first night that seemed like it was a hundred years ago.

Something wasn't so glorious this time. Something wasn't so splendid. Now, I saw that beautiful dress, and the comely shape it adorned, were just a cheap costume for the sordid darkness that dwelt within.

Although she didn't seem particularly surprised to see Bigelow, her eyes became as wide as watches when she saw me. Her face looked even paler than it had this morning.

"Preston?" she gasped.

"That's right. I'm the guy you keep trying to get rid of."

Bigelow pointed the gun at her. Something within me – perhaps the last vestige of chivalry I thought her beauty merited – prompted me to wrestle the rod out of his hand. When he lunged for it, I pounded him back so his head slammed off the brick wall and knocked him cold. I went into the dressing room with her.

“But, Preston,” Laura remonstrated as I locked the door. “I’ll be on in a few minutes.”

“We had a little deal, remember?” I sneered. “I was going into an empty house, and you were gonna wait for me until I came out.”

“I know, Preston, but I heard the gunfire, and, and I assumed the worst. I’m sorry, darling, I panicked. I thought, I thought – oh, I don’t know what I thought!”

She sat down in her chair and laid her arms on the vanity and began to sob.

“Skip it,” I snorted. "The gunfire didn’t surprise you. How could it, when you set me up to get plugged?”

“But I didn’t, Preston. I thought Murdoch would be gone. I thought he had gone with, with her.”

“How’d you know he wasn’t gone?”

Her pretty face turned white again, and she trembled. “Because, because you told me he was in there, didn’t you?”

I shook my head.

"Yes, Preston, you said Murdoch was inside. Or perhaps you don't remember. Is that a condition of your insanity, not being able to remember what you say or do?"

"My insanity, huh?" I stuck my hands into my pockets. "It's a little late for that gag, sister. But, you know, Murdoch did have some interesting information to share before your brutes bumped him off. He let me know this arranging for me to get put away was your idea. And so was paying off guys to make me think I'm insane. Because, being the upstanding racketeer he was, he didn't want to take credit for someone else's ingenuity."

"Preston, stop it," Laura sobbed. "Can't you see what your words are doing to me?"

"You're breaking my heart."

"Please don't be so cruel. You know I love you."

"You love me, huh? You've got a screwy way of showing it. A couple of beatdowns, a shower of bullets, and a trip to the nuthouse. I don't think I like that kind of love. I like the kind where you can depend on a girl to stick by you and not stab you in the back."

"You don't know what you're saying, sweet," Laura shook her pretty head. "The insanity is overwhelming you. You must go back to the asylum. You must go back to the place where you can be cured, where kind people will help remedy your madness."

“I should have let Bigelow give it to you out there, because getting the chair is too good for your kind. Maybe I should petition the D.A. to give you a taste of your own medicine. Yes, that's it. A nice stay at the nuthouse. It's really not as bad as it sounds. After a while, you might even get to liking it up there. You meet such interesting people.”

Laura whipped around with a revolver in her shapely right hand. The tears were gone; a murderous expression that reveled in violence flickered in their place.

“You’re sweet, darling, but you’re a little slow in deduction. Certainly, I paid off Duryea and Schuler. I told Chandler to talk to you as if you were insane. I even sent Feet and Mitts to give you a shakedown. I extracted much pleasure from it, Preston. You were so sure I loved you, weren't you? 'Darling, I want to be with you from now on. I don’t want to ever be apart from you anymore. You see, I love you.' Don't you remember that I'm an actress?"

"You'd be poison whether you were an actress or not."

"Manipulating you into following a false trail was particularly pleasant. Nigel had mentioned you often enough that I knew you would be suspicious if anything happened to him, so I had Duryea follow you the day after you went to the police station. The rest was quite simple to arrange, especially with Chandler’s influence. A shame his usefulness expired, but I couldn't have him alive and armed with incriminating information against me. I should be grateful Feet and Mitts' marksmanship was more accurate than when they chased you here."

"Did those goons bump off Nigel?"

"Nigel? Oh, poor, darling Preston. You think everything was about Nigel, don't you? Do you know what Nigel was, dearest? Nigel was a sucker that got too close to the fly trap. He thought I loved him – I couldn't if I tried, not that I would try – and that was all the sap wanted. He even agreed to cut off contact with everyone he knew, because we were going to 'lead a new life together.' As soon as I found out what he wanted from Whit, I saw what high purpose he would have."

So that was why Nigel had told me so little about her. That was why he had cut off contact with everyone who knew him. It was all part of her putrid plan. Nigel was just a pawn in her sordid game.

"What was your problem with Bigelow?"

"Whit always treated me as if I wasn't anything but his handmaid. Nobody treats me that way, not even if he's as important as Whit. I broke off the relationship, but that wasn't my revenge. The first step was pretending there was a rare jade. It was very easy to convince Whit the jade was worth getting and Chandler cooperated, since he thought I would marry him if he helped me get rid of Whit. I played them all against each other, you see? Whit jealous of Nigel, Nigel fearful of Whit, Chandler suspicious of what Nigel would find out. And they all did it, because they thought they would get me."

"You're despicable," I muttered without the Daffy Duck accent.

"Mind your manners, darling," Laura sneered. "Remember, I'm the one holding the gun."

She glanced down at the gun, then smiled at me. That smile had lost all its luster.

"You killed Nigel."

"The plan was always for Whit to kill him, which he would have done if more time had passed. But Nigel was beginning to figure things out, and that would have proved troublesome. You and that blundering uncle of mine thought I was in here that night, but I wasn't. Nigel had come to my apartment that afternoon. He said he didn't care about his art anymore; all he cared about was me. I pretended to be touched. You've seen my performance before."

"It makes me sick."

"I told him to get some money wherever he could and meet me here after the play. The dope didn't know what was coming. Even though I had to set one of my cars aflame, I enjoyed it. I enjoyed it very much. Even let him roll around and make some calls – to you, I believe. You see, Preston, if he had lived and told what he knew, not even my beauty and charm would neutralize Whit. It was simply a matter of value – Nigel's life, or my freedom. It wasn't hard to choose."

She giggled to herself and rubbed the edge of the gun with her fingertips. Calling me all those times had been Nigel's last gasp.

"I like to toy with my prey, Preston," she continued. "There's a stimulation to exerting power over others' lives, particularly weak fools who follow whatever I say. Don't be angry with me, Preston. As I said, Whit would have killed Nigel eventually, so long as he thought he was holding out on him."

She was evil, evil to the core. Pure, unadulterated evil, undefiled by even the slightest trace of goodness. Her grief for Nigel's death had been an act. Her affection for me had been an act. Her every word and move had been an act, down to welling up at me for mentioning Nigel's name.

"Diversion is a magician's finest trick," she gloated. "You were so occupied with Whit and Chandler and Amelia that you forgot about me. I wish you had stayed occupied with them, really, I do. A darling like you could have done wonders for me. But don't look so uneasy, sweet. The police will be here soon to take you back to where you belong. I called them as soon as I heard you speaking to Whit. What, you thought I was doing my hair and putting on my dress? Hah! The world is full of fools."

There was a knock at the door.

"It's the law!" a rough voice snarled.

"Ah, right on schedule," Laura smiled and kept the gun trained on me while unlocking the door.

Only, it wasn't the law; it was Bigelow. He smiled and emptied his cannister on Laura. The wicked flickering vanished from her eyes for the last time. It was all over with her, just like that.

Some girl, Laura. A double-crossing murderess that had killed my friend without thinking twice. A sweet talking slaughterer that duped me with the routine, just like she'd duped a dozen dopes before me.

Nigel, Murdoch, Bigelow, myself – she had made suckers of us all.

24

TOMORROW IS ANOTHER DAY

Bigelow blew the tip of his gun and gave me a glance.

"Do you approve, Mr. Welles?"

I was in too much shock to respond with anything besides a slight tilt of my head.

"Innovation is a trademark of the Bigelows," he sat down at the vanity. "I had a very high opinion of Laura, in spite of herself. After all, she was my old flame. Her charm was practically irresistible. But a man can only take so much."

Bigelow sniffed the carnation in his pocket and glanced at me. "I don't particularly like you, Mr. Welles, but I respect your resolve. I regard you as one befitting of Horace's line, 'A man just and steadfast in purpose.' Something truly noble is required for a man to do what you did to find out about his friend, something most men do not have and do not want to have. You are beaten repeatedly, you meet with a multitude of dead end clues, you are institutionalized, but you persist in your quest for the truth. That is honor. That is character."

Bigelow took a cigar out of his front pocket and lit it. "I intended to leave you with the blame, since you seem to have experience with that sort of thing. But the law would institutionalize you again without a second thought, and I found that possibility most disagreeable. I do not have as much influence over them as you think, but I shall pull my levers sufficient to make you a free man."

"Why?" I frowned, still in some shock.

"Haven't you been listening? I respect you, Mr. Welles. I respect you so thoroughly I pretended to be unconscious so you could draw information from Laura while I listened."

"Don't do this if you expect me to start doing you favors."

"A man does not always desire to receive something in return for a good deed. Your friend Wilfred wasn't a bad sort. He just had a weakness many of us have – vulnerability to the charms of a seductress."

"Why'd Nigel go to your office the night he was killed?"

"I arranged to meet him," Bigelow puffed. "He was supposed to have the jade, but I heard whispers from a couple of Murdoch's affiliates that he had sold it. Then, Laura called me that afternoon and told me he planned on running away with her that night. That seemed possible, but I was suspicious. Naturally, I wanted to learn what his plans really were. He told me he had never stolen the jade and that he wasn't going to look for it anymore because his art wasn't as important to him as Laura was. We had a drink, and he left. I might have sent Neville after him eventually, but not then. I surmised if he truly had the jade, he would not have agreed to see me. When I heard he was dead, I suspected Laura told Murdoch to tell the press what to say about it."

I had come out of my shock enough to begin comprehending what had happened. It didn't seem possible. It didn't seem real.

"But you acted like you were hiding something," I muttered. "And your barkeep acted like you were behind it."

"Perhaps he thought I was," Bigelow shrugged. "I was content with people thinking I was involved, if that was what was necessary for Laura to return to me. But neither of us got what we wanted. Nigel did not get his art displayed. I did not get the jade. And neither of us got her."

"Just the way she wanted it," I muttered. "Except for your bumping her off."

Voices in the hallway rose above the music and drew nearer. The square-jawed man entered with a very unpleasant look, followed by Malden and Dixon and several stiff-backed cops in full uniform.

"Bigelow?" the square-jawed man scowled. "What are you doing here?"

"Some business required my attention," Bigelow replied with a smile.

"And Welles," the square-jawed man said. "You did this, didn't you?"

"Of course he did," Dixon spat. "The punk killed Wilfred, the punk attacked Murdoch, the punk attacked the queen in the asylum, and now the punk killed this dame."

"Didn't you hear, copper?" I smirked at the square-jawed man. "I'm a violent lunatic."

"Don't talk to the chief like that, you swine," Dixon growled as he swung a wild punch at me. I sidestepped the blow with ease, but doing so wasn't necessary. After all those fists and feet and drugs, what was another smack?

"Mr. Welles is innocent," Bigelow stood while tapping the ashes from his cigar onto the floor. "Laura was holding him at gunpoint when I entered, prompting me to shoot her in self-defense. I have it on good authority that she murdered Wilfred and arranged for Chandler Murdoch to be shot earlier this evening. And as we speak, two of her brutes are roaming about the neighborhood. It would be advisable for you to capture them."

"I don't believe it for a second," the square-jawed man huffed. "But even if all that's true, Welles is still coming with us. The D.A. petitioned for him to be institutionalized, and that means he belongs with the rest of the nuts."

"They should see Murdoch's laptop," I told Bigelow. "It proves that he set me up. There are e-mails showing he was a scam artist and a racketeer, and unedited recordings of him admitting he was framing me for insanity because he wanted me out of the way. I was supposed to get the laptop tonight, only Laura double-crossed me."

"You see, gentlemen," Bigelow said, "there is no reason for alarm. I shot this murderous woman in self-defense, and Mr. Welles was framed for insanity by a proven quack who was following her orders."

I pulled my phone out of my pocket and revealed I had been recording audio since I had come into the theater.

"Mr. Welles is a genius," Bigelow smiled. "Such a shame he isn't interested in lending his talents to my business. I envision him as a great contributor to the restoration of antiquity and neoclassicism. We would make a very productive pair."

"Give me that phone, punk," Dixon flung his paws at it.

"Not until I get assurance I won't be going back to that nuthouse."

"We can't give you that," the square-jawed man snorted. "Even if we wanted to – and I'll assure you we *don't* want to – that's for the state to decide."

"Don't be absurd," Bigelow snickered. "You'll let him go now, or I shall rethink our rules of engagement. You have benefited from a favorable deal for a very considerable time. I give you twice as much as I give the state police, yet you don't even thank me."

The square-jawed man blushed, then scowled again and angrily shook his head. He glanced at Malden, then at Dixon, then at me.

"You win, Bigelow. But you'd better start giving us our cut on schedule. We haven't even gotten last month's earnings yet."

"I will," Bigelow said. "Now tell my man Welles he's free to go."

The square-jawed man gave me a dirty look. "You're free to go," he snarled.

"Desire anything else from them, Mr. Welles?" asked Bigelow.

"Issue a correction to your previous verdict on Nigel and admit he had been killed by Laura. Give him a public exoneration."

"Did you hear that, gentlemen?" Bigelow asked the cops. "You'd best make it clear that Nigel Wilfred was a stupendous artist who was double-crossed by a conniving murderess, and nothing else."

"We'll make it clear," the square-jawed man snapped.

"Fine," Bigelow smiled. "Come by The Parthenon again, Mr. Welles. I shall be featuring some of Wilfred's work, and I'd like to solicit your input on which pieces to display."

So, I was free to go. The law would need to get Murdoch's laptop and verify my story for themselves, then pair that with my audio recording of Laura before the case would be officially closed, but I was free to go. I was free to arrange Nigel's funeral and ask Mrs. Hattie permission to go through his things and retrieve his paintings from Laura's house.

Now that everything was finished, the tears came out again accordingly. It was a different variation on grief's theme than I had experienced at the beginning of it all, when the shock and confusion pulled different strings on my heart. This was simple rue, plain regret, honest sorrow, ordinary melancholy.

"Find your playmates, Jack?" the kid in the scarlet uniform smirked as I trudged through the corridor.

"Unlock the door."

"Indecisive, aren't you, Jack? You come in here wanting the door closed, and now you want it open. You know, extra service like that don't come free, Jack."

"You got your dough already. Fifty for letting me in, and fifty for letting me out."

"Smart mathematics, Jack."

"You'll be staying in here after you let me out. I've seen enough of you for a lifetime."

"Appreciate the compliment, Jack."

I was still winded and weary, so I sat on the top concrete step and thought about *Artist's Life* and Nigel, thought of our shared mirth and shared desires and shared hopes and shared joys, thought of a thousand occasions like the one in the bakery last Christmas, thought of his encouraging words when I was down and his good sense when I needed it. I thought of his pocket watch, and his paintings, and that little spot along the Connecticut River of which he had spoken so warmly.

Perhaps I would go there to absorb the sights and sounds that he had found pleasure in. He had thought I could write enough poems on that spot to fill a book. It was worth trying, but even if I did not write any about the scenery, I knew I would write many about my friend.

The door swung open. I didn't need another close up of the kid in the scarlet uniform, so I went down the stairs and kept staring at the brick wall directly east.

"I thought you'd went, Mr. Welles," said a voice like the sound of biting into a fresh apple. I turned around.

Bigelow extracted a cigar from his coat pocket as he leaned against the railing. He swiped a match on the door and poured a ponderous puff into the air.

“As I said, Mr. Welles, your friend Wilfred wasn’t a bad sort. Doubtless, he would still be alive, had he not the misfortune of falling under her spell.”

"His ambition was his undoing," I muttered. "He wasn't satisfied gradually building his career. He wanted to launch to the stratosphere too soon. I don't think he'd have met you, if he had been patient. I don't think he'd have met her, if he had been patient."

"Perchance. There was within him that singular spirit shared with Icarus, by which men's desires prompt them to fly too near the sun of their destruction. They have before them a realm of contentment and peaceful hopes, which they spurn to pursue the unattainable."

Bigelow shook his head and hurled the cigar out of view.

"Wilfred once told me," said he, "of a spot by the Connecticut River he delighted to observe, when ambition did not burn in his bosom. If only he had known that was real paradise, and the hopes of his heart for grandeur and renown but illusions."

Yes, if only he had known. If only he had known that murder and malice lurked within Laura Ridgley's heart. If only he had known death awaited him at the end of a path which promised prosperity. The world was a murk of cruel mystery.

But as I walked down the dark passage – a passage not half so dark as that pool I'd plunged into on the rainy night at Murdoch's – a glimmer of optimism glowed within my soul. Something convinced me that tomorrow is another day, that eventually this grief would crystallize into something sensible, that this bitter sorrow would breed wisdom by which I would profit all my days.

While I waited to learn the lessons of loss, I resolved to keep Nigel's memory aflame. And if I saw the morrow morn, I resolved to rise a sadder and a wiser man, as Coleridge's ancient mariner, with these words on my lips: Long live Nigel!

THE END